Excel

Get the Results You Want

Years 5–6
Selective Schools and Scholarship Writing Tests

Alan Horsfield

PASCAL
PRESS

© 2022 Alan Horsfield and Pascal Press

Completely new edition incorporating late 2020 Selective School test changes

Reprinted 2024

ISBN 978 1 74125 710 6

Pascal Press Pty Ltd
PO Box 250
Glebe NSW 2037
(02) 9198 1748
www.pascalpress.com.au

Publisher: Vivienne Joannou
Project editor: Mark Dixon
Edited by Mark Dixon
Answers checked by Dale Little
Cover by DiZign Pty Ltd
Typeset by Grizzly Graphics (Leanne Richters)
Printed by Vivar Printing/Green Giant Press

Contents

Writing—Cloze tests

Writing—Spelling tests

ABOUT THIS BOOK

The first part of this book focuses on practising various writing skills. These include:

Cloze exercises

These are questions where you have to fill in the missing words.

Read the title and the whole passage before trackling cloze exercises.

Example: Getting to work each day, Dr Cheng always ___**1**___ the bus because there was a bus stop directly in front of her house.

l.   A   raced
     B   drove
     C   caught
     D   catching

Option D is wrong because it is grammatically incorrect. Although all other answers **may** be possible, the only answer that is really appropriate is C.

Sometimes the answer will become obvious **later** in the passage. Look at this sentence:

On his way through the dark ___**2**___, Brett tried to keep his balance.

2.   A   hall
     B   lane
     C   tunnel
     D   forest

All options could be right—until you read on. The next sentence is:

Large protruding roots kept tripping him up.

Option D then becomes the most appropriate choice.

Spelling exercises

These are simple tests to see how well you spell or edit. They usually depend upon recognition of incorrectly spelt words.

See page 18 for details.

Editing exercises

In these exercises you will be expected to recognise mistakes in spelling, word usage, grammar or punctuation.

Because of the nature of language, testing is rarely confined to just one particular aspect. In any sentence there may be opportunities for those setting the tests to examine your understanding of grammar, punctuation, spelling and comprehension.

Dictionary exercises

Such exercises can relate to all forms of word study and word understanding. Emphasis is on alphabetical (dictionary) order.

Vocabulary exercises

These test how well you understand words in context, i.e. how they are used in sentences and passages. See page 38 for details.

Punctuation exercises

These will test your understanding of full stops, commas, question marks, dashes, exclamation marks, semicolons and inverted commas.

Grammar exercises

These will test your knowledge of grammar rules.

The second part of this book focuses on test practice: there are four sample Writing tests.

Students are given a writing task to complete. A tips page is provided for each question to support the student in their writing. When the student has completed their piece of writing, a sample piece of writing is provided to help them mark their work. Please note these writing samples have not been written by Year 5 or 6 students under test conditions.

BACKGROUND TO SELECTIVE TESTING

Tests for entry into selective government schools were introduced in order to provide an opportunity for pupils with scholastic aptitude. Over 15 000 applications are made for the just over 4000 selective places available and entry is quite competitive. It is not unusual for some primary schools not to be able to place even one of their pupils into a selective school.

The tests were updated in 2020 with a greater emphasis on literacy, critical-thinking skills, mathematical reasoning and problem solving. The General Ability Test has been replaced by a Thinking Skills Test. The new NSW Selective High School Placement Test adjusts and balances the weighting given to the Reading, Thinking Skills, Mathematical Reasoning and Writing components. These changes were in response to the findings of the 2018 Review of Selective Education Access report, commissioned by the NSW Department of Education.

ABOUT THE SELECTIVE SCHOOL TEST

The NSW Selective High School Placement Test consists of four sections:

Reading (30 questions in 40 minutes)
Mathematical Reasoning (35 questions in 40 minutes)
Thinking Skills (40 questions in 40 minutes)
Writing (one question in 30 minutes).

The tests, except Writing, are in multiple-choice form, with each question being of equal value. Marks are awarded for each correct answer and applicants are advised to guess the answer if they are uncertain.

Although there are similarities in the content of the NSW Selective High School Placement Test and the ACER Scholarship Tests, since the Selective School Tests format was changed in 2020 there are now more differences. The next section looks at the background to the ACER Scholarship Tests.

HOW THE RESULTS ARE USED BY PUBLIC SCHOOLS

Entry to selective high schools is based on academic merit. In 2022 changes were made to the allocation of places. Under the Equity Placement Model, up to 20% of places are held for members of the following disadvantaged and under-represented groups:

- students from low socio-educational advantage backgrounds
- First Nations students
- rural and remote students
- students with disability.

It is important to remember that the places allocated under the Equity Placement Model will not necessarily be filled. In 2023, the first year of this new system, less than 10% of these places were offered. This means that more than 90% of the places were offered to general applicants. The new system has helped close the educational gap in participation from disadvantaged groups without having a significant impact on other applicants.

Students no longer receive a test score or placement rank. The new performance report will instead place students in one of the following categories:

- top 10% of candidates
- next 15% of candidates
- next 25% of candidates
- lowest 50% of candidates.

This change addresses privacy and wellbeing concerns including unhealthy competition between students. The sole purpose of the test is to identify students who would benefit from the chance to study at a selective school and, since it doesn't test knowledge of the curriculum, there is no diagnostic merit in the test—unlike the NAPLAN test, which can help identify areas where children can improve.

Minimum entry scores for selective schools are no longer published because these change from year to year and depend on the number of applicants, their relative performance and the number of families who decline an offer. Students placed on the reserve list no longer receive a numerical rank; instead an indication of how long it will take to receive an offer, based on previous years, is provided.

A selection committee for each selective high school decides which students are to be offered places. These committees also decide how many students are to be placed on the reserve list. Should a student with a confirmed offer turn down a place at a selective school, the place will be offered to the first student on the reserve list.

There is an appeals panel for illness or other mitigating circumstances. All applicants are advised of the outcome. The NSW Government provides detailed information on the application and selection process for parents on the Selective High School Placement Test. This is available from: https://education.nsw.gov.au/parents-and-carers/learning/tests-and-exams/selective-school-test.

Sample test papers are also available on this website.

ABOUT THE SCHOLARSHIP TESTS

The ACER Scholarship Tests, which are usually held around May, are coordinated by the Australian Council for Educational Research (ACER). This testing is for entry to around 200 independent schools. About 15 000 students throughout Australia sit these tests.

The tests cover three levels:
- Level 1: the last year of primary school (Year 6)
- Level 2: the second year of high school (Year 8)
- Level 3: Year 10 in high school.

Each private school awards its own scholarships. You can put your name down for more than one school but you will need a special registration form. There is also a separate fee for each school and you lodge your registration directly with the school and not with ACER.

You may be limited in the number of schools to which you can apply. This might happen if a school insists you have to take the test at their testing centre. Candidates usually take the exam at the school which is their first choice.

There are exceptions for country and interstate candidates. The ACER Scholarship Tests comprise:
- Test 1: Written Expression (25 minutes)
- Test 2: Humanities—Comprehension and Interpretation (40 minutes)
- Test 3: Mathematics (40 minutes)
- Test 4: Written Expression (25 minutes).

HOW THE RESULTS ARE USED BY PRIVATE SCHOOLS

The results are used by private schools to select students who have applied for a scholarship. Typically the highest scorers are considered first, together with any additional background information that might have been provided. It is important therefore to provide as much detail as possible in the application form to assist the selection committee in deciding between pupils who may have similar scores.

ADVICE FOR IMAGINATIVE WRITING

Good creative writing

Alan Horsfield, as a former President and Development Officer for the Children's Book Council (NSW Branch), has some hints for good creative writing. Note: This is not for information reports or persuasive writing.

Alan's eleven top recommendations

1. You can become a competent writer just as you can become a competent runner, driver or softball player. You need to practise. The more you practise, the better you will get.
2. Enter your work in competitions. Competitions make you more critical of

your own efforts. The competitions may be for anything from your school's yearbook to writing competitions run by the local council or bookshop.

3. Don't be afraid of making mistakes. Even some of the greatest authors have boxes of rejected manuscripts—and boxes of pages that didn't even reach a publisher.

4. If you have an idea you want to write about, no matter how silly it seems, run with it. Some of the world's best books seem a little silly when reduced to a few words. Who would have thought that a book about a talking pig would have made millions?

5. Read a lot of books on the subject you are interested in. If you want to write science fiction, read what other successful authors have written. Your idea might have been used by another author—but then you might be able to tell the story in a much more interesting way!

6. Let your imagination run freely.

7. Don't forget your personal experiences are a very important source of information.

8. Keep a notebook where you can write ideas you might (or might not) use later. Very few of us can trust memory to make these ideas resurface. One day that idea or incident might develop into a story. Paddington Bear, for instance, had a very simple beginning.

9. When you are burning with an idea to write about, don't worry about spelling, full stops, capital letters, margins, pictures, and so on. These can be dealt with later. The ideas may disappear forever if you let them go.

10. Don't worry about starting with a title. That can come when you have written the story every filmmaker wants to turn into a miniseries.

11. Make sure you own a dictionary and a thesaurus, and try to meet successful authors whenever possible!

ADVICE TO PARENTS/ GUARDIANS

Every child has their own talents which need to be discovered and nurtured. Some children are high achievers or have special talents which are not reflected in the results of these tests.

This is because these tests focus on predicting the overall educational achievement of high scorers but may not be accurate in predicting how well a particular pupil might perform. In fact some pupils with high scores in these tests may not ultimately do well in high school while some who were not selected will go on to attain excellent academic results.

Children need to be interested in undertaking these tests. This will be a significant and memorable event for them and they need support as the tests are very competitive.

It is advisable that children should not undertake the NSW Selective High School Placement Test unless some of the following criteria are satisfied:

- they are among the top of their class at school
- they attend an Opportunity Class
- they are very good at English and Mathematics
- they read widely
- it is their decision to apply for a selective school
- the preparation for the test is not stressful for them.

This book is designed to give an opportunity for your child to become familiar with the format and style of the test questions.

Suggested procedure:
- Complete the first test.
- Keep a record of your times and accuracy.
- Repeat each test until you get **all** the questions correct.
- Keep on repeating each test until you are familiar with it.

- Keep on repeating each test until the time it takes you to finish the test is as fast as possible.
- Now repeat this with the next test.
- Then, when you are confident, you can complete the next test.

Keep in mind that some question types may require more practice than others. You might need more time initially to complete these sorts of questions. Some of the more challenging Thinking Skills problem-solving questions, for example, could take you up to 15 minutes to complete to begin with, as you may use diagrams or tables to help you solve them. Remember that the more questions you do of this same type, the faster you will become—until you know exactly how to solve them.

ADVICE TO STUDENTS

The tests are difficult and you may not finish them in the time available. Don't worry about this because many students will also find the questions very hard. You can't learn the answers to the questions in these tests like you can with some school tests because they force you to deal with new situations.

We wish you all the best in the tests and hope these notes will be of some help in making you familiar with the different types of questions in the test and helping you increase your speed and accuracy. Don't worry if you don't get a place because there are thousands and thousands of applicants. Just give it your best shot.

Here is a summary of the advice that the Education Department and ACER give to people taking the tests:

- There is nothing special that you have to learn in order to do these tests.
- These are tests to see whether you can think clearly with words and numbers.
- Listen carefully to the instructions.
- If you are not sure what to do then ask.

- Make sure you know where to mark the answers for each test.
- Do not open the test booklet until you are told.
- Read each question carefully before giving your answer.
- There is no penalty for guessing—so guess if you are not sure.
- Don't rush—work steadily and as carefully as you can.
- If a question is too hard, don't worry—come back to it later if you have time.
- It is easy to get your answers out of order, so always check the number of the question you are answering.
- Every now and then make sure the answer is in the correctly numbered circle.
- Feel free to write on the question booklet for any rough working.
- Don't do any rough work on the answer sheet.
- If you want to change an answer, rub it out and fill in the appropriate circle for your new answer.
- Keep track of the time—you will not be told when time is running out.
- Don't fold the answer sheet—it has to be put through a machine to mark it.

For the NSW Selective High School Placement Test you will need:
- a good pencil rubber (one that doesn't smudge)
- a HB or B pencil (don't use pens or biros)
- a spare pencil.

For the ACER Scholarship Tests you will need:
- a good pencil rubber (one that doesn't smudge)
- a HB or B pencil (for the answer sheet)
- a spare pencil
- two blue or black pens for the Writing Test.

SELECTIVE SCHOOL–STYLE TEST **Writing—Cloze tests**

MINI TEST 1: Recount

Cloze exercises test how well you understand or comprehend a written passage. They test your understanding of parts of speech, correct usage and grammar.

For example: He should _____ gone home after school.

Possible choices: **A** of **B** off **C** had **D** have D is correct.

They may also test spelling:

For example: The students have done _____ homework.

Possible choices: **A** there **B** they're **C** their **D** thier C is correct.

Trapped in a thundercloud

US Marine Pilot William Rankin had the adventure of his life in 1959. His plane went out of control during a bad storm. He had to bail out at 14 000 metres with a parachute.

Rankin hoped to **1** _____ gently to earth. Instead he found himself right in the middle of a big, black storm cloud. The winds inside the cloud swept him up, dropped him **2** _____ a stomach-churning lurch and bounced him from side to side.

3 _____ and hailstones pelted him. The flashes of lightning were so bright that he had to squeeze his eyes shut. The thunder was a deep rumble **4** _____ made his body shake.

Finally the storm began to die down and Rankin **5** _____ his trip to earth. His terrifying ride through the **6** _____ took forty minutes.

It left him with a few bruises and an amazing story to tell.

By David Suzuki

For questions 1 to 6, choose the answer which best fits the meaning and style of the passage.

1 **A** drop
B float
C tumble
D fly

2 **A** in
B over
C with
D through

3 **A** Dust
B Rain
C Rocks
D Sticks

4 **A** but
B and
C that
D what

5 **A** got
B had
C began
D finished

6 **A** thundercloud
B lightning
C night
D hail

MINI TEST 2: Explanation

Bats

While birds rule the daytime skies, the bat—a flying mammal—is master of the air at night.

Its leathery wings are strong and efficient for flying. They are made of **1** _____ skin flaps that stretch between the incredibly long fingers of the bat's hand. During the day, most bats usually roost in large groups in caves, attics or hollow trees, hanging upside down with **2** _____ clawed hind feet.

Most bats go hunting at night for food such as moths but some have different ways of feeding. Vampire bats from Central and South America feed on the blood of people, cows and horses. Fruit bats, sometimes called **3** _____ foxes, feed on the fruit of tropical trees. Hunting bats catch mice on the ground or fish that swim near the **4** _____ of a lake.

Bats have a clever way of finding their food in complete darkness. They detect their **5** _____ using a system called echolocation. The bat sends out very high-pitched noises (ultrasonic sounds) that 'echo' or bounce **6** _____ its prey. Using the echoes to locate its prey, the bat then **7** _____, captures and eats it.

Like some birds, some bats have learned to live in large colonies in many big cities.

By J Kelly & Dr P Whitfield

For questions 1 to 7, choose the answer which best fits the meaning and style of the passage.

1
A durable
B bright
C delicate
D flexible

2
A its
B his
C their
D there

3
A wild
B little
C night
D flying

4
A bottom
B shores
C surface
D overflow

5
A prey
B cave
C flock
D enemies

6
A off
B from
C near
D over

7
A kills
B traps
C chases
D catches

The St Bees Man

One of the loneliest and most beautiful places in England is St Bees Head on the coast of Cumbria.

The monks **1** _____ lived there are long gone but for six hundred years a most unusual preserved person lay hidden **2** _____ a secret vault under their church.

In 1981 an archaeologist called Deidre O'Sullivan **3** _____ the skeletons of many medieval monks when she noticed a strange slope in the ground where she was working. The slope led her to a sandstone crypt or vault set in the ground near what was once an altar of the church.

Deidre O'Sullivan climbed **4** _____ into the crypt to investigate. Lying on the dusty floor was a skeleton and the rotted remains of an ancient wooden **5** _____ . She grew very **6** _____ . Although only a few rusted fastenings were left of the wooden coffin, beneath the clay packing which had **7** _____ it she could see a second, lead coffin in the shape of a human body.

Lead coffins of this **8** _____ had not been used since medieval times, around AD 1300.

Whose body could the coffin contain? The coffin was taken to the surface, where it was cut open. Two shrouds were removed—to reveal the open mouth and staring eyes of a medieval knight.

By Natalie Jane Prior

For questions 1 to 8, choose the answer which best fits the meaning and style of the passage.

1
A who
B that
C what
D which

2
A on
B in
C near
D under

3
A broken
B concealed
C uncovered
D disclosed

4
A up
B over
C down
D across

5
A box
B alter
C table
D coffin

6
A tired
B excited
C thoughtful
D frightened

7
A filled
B broken
C covered
D preserved

8
A age
B size
C type
D colour

St Bees Priory Church

MINI TEST 4: Report

Mystery of the *Mary Celeste*

Sailors have always told stories of sea monsters, huge storms and times when there wasn't the slightest breath of wind.

They also tell tales of mystery ships: **1** _____ ships which suddenly appear and disappear, and ships which sail with ghost crews or no crews at all. One of the **2** _____ of these tales is the story of the *Mary Celeste*.

The story began as a speck on the horizon somewhere in the Atlantic Ocean on 4 December 1872. As the speck got closer and **3** _____ larger, Captain Morehouse of the ship *Dei Gratia* became curious. He could see the ship's sails were set but the ship was changing course **4** _____ every gust of wind. Sometimes it veered to the right, sometimes it veered to the left, then to the right again. For no sensible reason. Something was **5** _____.

Sailing closer, Morehouse **6** _____ through his telescope. He read the name of the ship: *Mary Celeste*. He knew the vessel: only a month ago in New York, he had met the captain, Benjamin Briggs. Captain Briggs, his wife Sarah, baby daughter Sophia and a crew of eight had set sail on the ship—along with a cargo of 1700 casks of crude alcohol.

Morehouse could see the wheel of the ship was turning freely but no-one was steering it. More alarming still there was nobody on deck. In fact, there appeared to be no sign of **7** _____ on board at all. Where were the captain and crew?

He ordered several of his own sailors to board the *Mary Celeste*, her torn sails **8** _____ in the breeze. The sailors checked the ship thoroughly but there was no sign of life. The captain's log book was still in the right place but the lifeboat, ship's papers and navigational instruments were all missing.

The crew searched the logbook for clues but what they found there only added to the mystery.

By Noeline Martin

For questions 1 to 8, choose the answer which best fits the meaning and style of the passage.

1
A small
B ghost
C motor
D foreign

2
A oldest
B latest
C strangest
D greatest

3
A seemed
B become
C loomed
D emerged

4
A by
B in
C with
D under

5
A lost
B wrong
C broken
D unusual

6
A peered
B peeped
C watched
D glanced

7
A life
B cargo
C ghosts
D welcome

8
A rigid
B stretched
C dangling
D flapping

MINI TEST 5: Poetry

Clowns

Zing! goes the cymbal. Bang! goes the drum,
See how they tipple-topple-tumbling come,
Dazing the country, dazzling the towns,
1 _____ the procession of the circus clowns.
Hop on the heel and twist on the **2** _____,
See how they wibble-wabble-waddling go.
Bim-bam-balloons in clear blue air!
Clowns on the **3** _____ to they-don't-know-where.
Painted-on-smiles that are long and loud
Beam at the giggle-goggling **4** _____.
Under the **5** _____ do they grin so gay?
Nobody sees **6** _____ I just can't say.
Look how the clowns all a-cantering **7** _____
Riding their donkeys with a hee-haw-hum.
Where do they come from? Where do they go?
They kin-can't say for they din-don't know.

By Margaret Mahy

For questions 1 to 7, choose the answer which best fits the meaning and style of the passage.

1
A Heres
B Hears
C Here's
D How's

2
A toe
B sole
C shoe
D heel

3
A bus
B run
C march
D procession

4
A team
B crowd
C cloud
D spectators

5
A hats
B paint
C balloons
D perspiration

6
A so
B yet
C but
D although

7
A hum
B drum
C come
D strum

12 MIN

MINI TEST 6: Explanation

Extinction—dead as a dinosaur

Dinosaurs ruled the earth for about 160 million years. That's a very long time when you think that human beings, as we know them today, have only been around for one million years.

Dinosaurs died out and disappeared **1** _____ our planet 65 million years ago. This dying-out process is called extinction. Dinosaurs took several million years to become **2** _____ but considering they had been here for such a long time, they disappeared quite **3** _____.

Scientists are not exactly sure what caused dinosaurs to become extinct. Some scientists believe a huge meteorite from space **4** _____ into earth, sending up an enormous cloud of dust. This thick layer kept out the sun's rays, which stopped the plants from **5** _____. The plant-eating dinosaurs had nothing to eat and died out. In turn, the meat-eating dinosaurs also starved to death.

A layer of clay containing a substance called iridium, which is only found in outer space, has been **6** _____ in different parts of the world. By testing the clay, scientists discovered it was the same age as the **7** _____ that would have settled after the meteorite crash.

Those scientists who do not agree with this theory ask why only dinosaurs died and not other animals. They also **8** _____ why no huge graveyards filled with dinosaur bones have been found.

Other scientists believe the temperature of the world became colder and the new weather conditions did not suit the dinosaurs. Changes of climate could have been caused by land movements, a shift in the position of the North and South Poles, and changes to the way the earth spins round.

For questions 1 to 8, choose the answer which best fits the meaning and style of the passage.

1
A in
B off
C over
D from

2
A old
B lost
C extinct
D forgotten

3
A strangely
B quickly
C slowly
D early

4
A fell
B dropped
C crashed
D clashed

5
A seeding
B growing
C flowering
D germinating

6
A buried
B hidden
C observed
D discovered

7
A dust
B clay
C bones
D iridium

8
A say
B think
C explain
D question

12 MIN

MINI TEST 7: Explanation

While you sleep

Doctors used to think that people who walked in their sleep were acting out their dreams. But this has been proved untrue.

In 1952 researchers learnt that when we **1** _____, our eyes move rapidly under closed lids. **2** _____ show that everyone dreams every night. But we do not dream the whole time. Dreams occur when we're sleeping lightly but seldom when we're sleeping deeply. It was found that sleepwalkers are only active during deep sleep. They are not **3** _____ at the time.

An expert who has researched sleepwalking tells of a **4** _____ case. A college student would get up in her sleep. She would dress and walk a kilometre **5** _____ a river. There she would have a swim, then walk back to college and go back to bed. Like most sleepwalkers she couldn't recall doing any of those things.

There are reports **6** _____ sleepwalkers driving cars, buying a ticket and getting on a plane, even climbing from one rooftop to the next.

People who are sleepwalking seem to be in a trance. If they are **7** _____, they may not answer. If they do, they may sound offhand, as though annoyed.

Doctors agree that sleepwalkers should be woken **8** _____. If startled, they could become confused or scared. The best way to wake them is to repeat their name calmly, again and again.

If sleepwalkers are left alone, they will usually return to their bed when they have finished what they are doing.

For questions 1 to 8, choose the answer which best fits the meaning and style of the passage.

1
A relax
B dream
C get tired
D sleepwalk

2
A Tests
B Books
C Reports
D Opinions

3
A acting
B walking
C sleeping
D dreaming

4
A strange
B watched
C confusing
D hopeless

5
A to
B by
C over
D along

6
A of
B by
C from
D explaining

7
A spoken to
B sleeping
C disturbed
D startled

8
A often
B gently
C quickly
D immediately

MINI TEST 8: Narrative

Staying alive in year five

Anyway, there we were, with all this string, and had to do something with it.

I'm not sure how we got the idea really. We thought of **1** _____ it around the outside of the school. Then we thought we could trail it across the playground, so that Miss Holland, or whoever found it, would pick it up and follow it to see where it led, and half an hour later they'd be still **2** _____ it. It was about then we realised that because it was a Tuesday afternoon, Miss Holland would be at a staff meeting. And **3** _____ it was after 3.30, Mrs Wilson and the office staff would have gone home.

Johnny didn't **4** _____ dare me and I didn't exactly dare him but I think I said I'd do it if he would, so somehow we more or less agreed to do it.

Then we got another **5** _____: to tie something on the end of the string, as a little surprise, like a treasure hunt. So we raced around the school having a quick look—we were already running short of **6** _____ and we eventually found a scraggy old bone that a dog must have brought in and chewed on for a while then half buried. It smelt a bit. So that seemed the right sort of surprise.

7 _____ got into Miss Holland's office easily—we just walked straight in. We pulled down the blind, even though it meant we wouldn't have much warning of anyone coming, and got to work. I tied the bone to one end of the **8** _____ and put it in the drawer of her desk. Then we started unwinding it.

We passed it through the handles of the desk, around the filing cabinets and through their drawers, over the fluorescent light, under the desk, between the legs of the chairs, in and out of the pot plants, through the document trays, under the rug and around the umbrella stand.

By John Marsden

For questions 1 to 8, choose the answer which best fits the meaning and style of the passage.

1
A running
B pulling
C placing
D dropping

2
A finding
B studying
C following
D collecting

3
A if
B when
C while
D because

4
A only
B really
C usually
D exactly

5
A idea
B dare
C piece
D string

6
A time
B ideas
C string
D breath

7
A I
B We
C The staff
D Mrs Wilson

8
A desk
B blind
C room
D string

Icelandic moonscape

Ted had always been fascinated by the harsh extremes of hot and cold coming together in one land. He had to see it for himself.

In August 1984 he left his home in Lancashire, England, on a solo journey that would take **1** _____ right across Iceland. He set himself the challenge of going on foot so he could **2** _____ the land at close quarters. All he carried was a pack on his back containing a small tent, spare clothes, food and a camping stove.

The 8000-kilometre walk began in the town of Seydisfjordur on the eastern side of the island **3** _____ ended in the capital city of Reykjavik on the west coast. Most of Iceland's small population of 180 000 people lived in Reykjavik. Nearly all his journey was across **4** _____ windswept moors and craggy spurs of twisted rock covered in ice and snow.

When Ted set out from Seydisfjordur it was autumn. Being so close to the Arctic Circle, the daylight began before six am and lasted well past eight o'clock in the evening. But the sun was weak and hid behind dark storm clouds which drenched Ted with rain as he **5** _____ onwards.

The land was bleak. Only **6** _____ people and their animals lived in this sort of climate. In one place he trekked across a desert of sharp lava rock that stretched as far as his eyes could see. There was no **7** _____ at all—not even a blade of grass.

The American astronauts in the Apollo program had trained in that spot a few years before. It was the closest thing on Earth to the landscape they would find when they arrived on the moon.

By Rick Wilson

For questions 1 to 7, choose the answer which best fits the meaning and style of the passage.

1
A all
B him
C them
D explorers

2
A watch
B enjoy
C endure
D experience

3
A and
B but
C yet
D then

4
A derelict
B deserted
C unoccupied
D uninhabited

5
A walked
B battled
C hurried
D straggled

6
A poor
B hardy
C elderly
D courageous

7
A vegetation
B villages
C shops
D roads

Iceland lava field

Creative puzzles of the world

Nearly all human beings love to test their wits on puzzles. There is an old tale about a young woman who, in a flash of insight, solved an apparently impossible problem.

Her father owed a large **1** _____to an evil moneylender and had no hope of paying it. The moneylender offered to release the father from his debt if he agreed to a wager.

The moneylender would **2** _____ a black pebble and a white one in a bag and the daughter would take one from it. If **3** _____ luck was good and she took the white pebble, the moneylender would make no claim against the father. However, **4** _____ she took the black pebble she would have to marry the moneylender. With no other choice available, the father **5** _____ the wager.

The moneylender picked up a handful of **6** _____ from the hundreds that were lying around. He dropped two in the bag—but the sharp-eyed daughter saw that they were both black.

Her dilemma was terrifying. She dared not expose the moneylender as a **7** _____ but she did not want to be compelled to marry him.

The girl turned the moneylender's trick against him in an ingenious way. She quickly took a pebble, fumbled in feigned nervousness, and dropped it before anyone could see its colour. It was immediately **8** _____ among the many pebbles on the ground.

'It's all right,' she said, 'we can easily find out what colour it was, for it was the opposite of the pebble that is still in the bag.' Thus she was able to 'prove' the pebble she had taken was actually white.

By Pieter van Delft & Jack Botermans

For questions 1 to 8, choose the answer which best fits the meaning and style of the passage.

1
A debt
B bill
C reward
D account

2
A hide
B place
C secure
D fasten

3
A the
B his
C her
D their

4
A if
B as
C when
D after

5
A encouraged
B approved
C agreed to
D allowed

6
A bags
B coins
C stones
D pebbles

7
A fool
B cheat
C trickster
D criminal

8
A safe
B lost
C hidden
D destroyed

The Triggerstone

As they watched, another section of the opposite bank sank down with a great bubbling and glurping from within.

'Run for it!' shouted Jefferson. They ran, stumbling, across the remains of the car park, catching up with the others as they stopped part way up the track.

They turned to **1** _____.

With a strange sucking noise, more and more of the historic site **2** _____ into the thick bubbling mud in the hole and was soon swallowed up.

Above they saw dense **3** _____, dipping lower, lower, and long streamers of dark air began to twirl in the pit. The cloud turned faster. The twisting column began to moan frighteningly.

The flat ground began to drop **4** _____ the pit in great chunks and shock waves went rippling across the bay. With each new collapse the earth let out a great Hurnk! sound, like someone would make when punching a punchbag. To Jinnie it **5** _____ like a very satisfied Hurnk!

Within **6** _____ half the site was gone and the edge of the hole was coming rapidly towards them. The moan of the tornado turned to a whistle and a fierce wind **7** _____ their clothing and threatened to blow them right **8** _____ their feet. Jinnie found herself holding on to Damien's arm with one hand and holding his hand with her other.

In the midst of all this noise and madness, he caught her eye and squeezed her hand gently. 'I'm sorry,' he said.

By Ged Maybury

For questions 1 to 8, choose the answer which best fits the meaning and style of the passage.

1
A rest
B watch
C relax
D escape

2
A sank
B buried
C floated
D descended

3
A air
B mud
C clouds
D streamers

4
A into
B onto
C around
D against

5
A felt
B looked
C seemed
D sounded

6
A instants
B seconds
C hours
D time

7
A pounded
B dirtied
C tore at
D ruffled

8
A of
B off
C from
D under

12 MIN

The Ghostly Door

The door had an ordinary, common black oblong lock with a brass knob. Dave tried the latch and found it fast; he turned the knob, opened the door and called, 'Puss—puss—puss!' but the cat wouldn't come.

He shut the **1** _____ , tried the knob to see that the catch had caught and got into bed again.

He'd scarcely settled down **2** _____ the door opened slowly, the black cat walked in, stared hard at Dave, and suddenly turned and darted out as the door closed smartly.

I **3** _____ at Dave and he looked at me—hard; then he scratched the back of his head. I never saw a man look so **4** _____ in the face and scared about the head.

He got out of bed very cautiously, took a **5** _____ of firewood in his hand, sneaked up to the door and snatched it open. There was no-one there. Dave took the candle and went into the next room **6** _____ couldn't see the cat. He came back and sat down by the fire and meowed, and **7** _____ the cat answered him and came in from somewhere—she'd been outside the window I suppose; he kept on meowing and she sidled up and rubbed against his hairy shin. Dave could generally bring a cat that way. He had a weakness for cats. He gave **8** _____ cat something to eat.

Then he went and held the light close to the lock on the door but could see nothing wrong with it. He found a **9** _____ on the mantle shelf and locked the door.

He got into bed again, and the cat jumped up and curled down at the foot and started her old drum going, like shot in a sieve. Dave bent down and patted her, to tell her he meant no harm when he stretched out his legs, and then he settled down again to read. He was reading *The Grisly Ghost of the Haunted Gulch*.

By Henry Lawson

For questions 1 to 9, choose the answer which best fits the meaning and style of the passage.

1
- **A** lock
- **B** knob
- **C** door
- **D** window

2
- **A** as
- **B** then
- **C** when
- **D** while

3
- **A** shouted
- **B** pointed
- **C** blinked
- **D** looked

4
- **A** understanding
- **B** puzzled
- **C** frantic
- **D** sorry

5
- **A** stick
- **B** block
- **C** bundle
- **D** weapon

6
- **A** but
- **B** yet
- **C** and
- **D** although

7
- **A** noiselessly
- **B** presently
- **C** purposely
- **D** abruptly

8
- **A** my
- **B** his
- **C** our
- **D** the

9
- **A** key
- **B** dish
- **C** lock
- **D** light

MINI TEST 13: Report

12 MIN

The Forgotten Thirteen

The first woman to go into space was Valentina Tereshkova of the Soviet Union in 1963.

In the United States the National Aeronautical and Space Administration (NASA) did not **1** _____ women to participate in the space program. Astronauts had to be **2** _____ of the army or air force, in which women were not allowed to become pilots. Thirteen women, all qualified pilots, had **3** _____ in 1960. All of them passed the medical tests, which they had arranged themselves, with the same doctor who had tested the men. But none of them was invited to join the program, though one, Jerrie Cobb, was hired as a 'consultant'—the most unconsulted consultant of any government body, she **4** _____! These became known as the 'Forgotten Thirteen'.

By 1978 things had changed. No-one had been to the **5** _____ for several years. The space program had simply become too expensive, and had to be made to pay for itself. Thus was born the space shuttle program. Reusable craft were used to take **6** _____ into space to launch and repair satellites, go to space stations and perform scientific experiments. Space shuttle crews usually consist of the pilot, mission specialist and a 'payload commander', who looks after the cargo which may be anything from **7** _____ to experimental plants.

The sixteenth of January 1978 was a turning point for women in the space program. **8** _____ that day NASA announced its latest intake of 35 astronauts. Of these, six were **9** _____ .

At the time the press took the whole business very lightly. 'Girls Out Of This World' said the headline of one Melbourne newspaper, with a cartoon in which a woman astronaut wanted to go back because she had run out of make-up. Yet all were highly educated scientists—a physicist, two doctors, a biochemist, an engineer and a geologist.

By Sue Bursztynski

For questions 1 to 9, choose the answer which best fits the meaning and style of the passage.

1
A need
B oppose
C allow
D entice

2
A representatives
B commanders
C members
D trainees

3
A tried
B entered
C enrolled
D succeeded

4
A hoped
B sighed
C smirked
D complained

5
A moon
B doctor
C government
D Soviet Union

6
A crews
B cadets
C women
D volunteers

7
A cargo
B repairs
C equipment
D consultants

8
A By
B On
C After
D Throughout

9
A men
B single
C women
D scientists

The Cosquer Cave

Beneath the surface, Henri Cosquer explained, was a cave—his own private cave, which he had discovered six years before, and which he had been exploring ever since.

The cave was one of the most dangerous he had ever **1** _____, which was one reason why he never told anyone about it. He suspected that the divers had accidentally found the entrance and come to grief **2** _____ the narrow passages beyond.

Cosquer and the rescue team put on their diving equipment and entered the tiny opening, little more than a metre high. Inside, pitch black had it not been for their torches, was a long **3** _____ passage. Clouds of silt were stirred up by the divers' flippers as they **4** _____ and the team quickly became disorientated. But Cosquer knew where he was going.

Soon, as he expected, they found the **5** _____ of the three missing divers. Now that his cave had been discovered and a tragedy had occurred, Cosquer knew the authorities would seal its entrance off to prevent further **6** _____. But before they did, he knew the cave's other **7** _____—the reason he'd been coming back for six whole years—would have to be shared with the rest of the world.

Signalling to the other divers, Henri Cosquer swam through a narrow **8** _____ in the rock at the end of the first passage. For six metres the divers wriggled through another passage **9** _____ over a metre high. At last, it opened out into another cave.

The divers swam past submerged stalagmites up to five metres high until their heads broke the surface in the middle of an underground lake.

Here, if only they had been able to find it, was the air that could have saved the other divers' lives.

By Natalie Jane Prior

For questions 1 to 9, choose the answer which best fits the meaning and style of the passage.

1
A saw
B seen
C enjoyed
D reported

2
A in
B under
C around
D through

3
A open
B bright
C narrow
D skinny

4
A past
B swim
C passed
D hurried

5
A trail
B bodies
C torches
D equipment

6
A crimes
B rescues
C accidents
D explorations

7
A entrance
B tragedy
C passage
D secret

8
A crack
B tunnel
C doorway
D depression

9
A just
B well
C only
D space

Magic squares

Every row, column and diagonal has a total of 15 and the numbers 1 to 9 have been used once only.

Apparently it was the ancient Chinese who first developed magic squares—those beautifully balanced arrays of numbers in which all rows, columns and diagonals add up to the same total.

6	7	2
1	5	9
8	3	4

According to Chinese legend, the first magic square appeared to the mythical **1** _____ Yu while he was walking beside the River Lo. The emperor spotted the **2** _____ in a pattern on the back of a tortoise. The traditional square was called *lo-shu*. It uses the numbers 1 to 9 once only and every row, column or diagonal adds up to 15 which is called the 'constant'. The constant can be found by adding **3** _____ the numbers from 1 to 9 and dividing by 3 as it is a 3 × 3 square. A 3 × 3 square is called an order three square.

To find the **4** _____ for an order four square, add the numbers 1 to 16 and divide by 4. The constant is 34.

To the Chinese the even numbers of the *lo-shu* represented the *yin* and the **5** _____ numbers represented the *yang*. Other groupings of numbers symbolise the five elements: earth, fire, metal, water and wood.

The study of magic squares **6** _____ from the Chinese to the Muslims and later to the Hindus. New methods were found. Muslims, like the Chinese, were able to find religious significance in magic squares. Europe became as fascinated by magic squares as Asia. In the 16th century the squares were still regarded as **7** _____ and were used for working spells.

Later, magic squares became a **8** _____ for mathematicians.

Benjamin Franklin, one of the Founding Fathers of the United States, amused himself by constructing them in his childhood. You could easily spend a lifetime on the delights of constructing magic squares.

By Pieter van Delft & Jack Botermans

For questions 1 to 8, choose the answer which best fits the meaning and style of the passage.

1
A mathematician
B historian
C emperor
D traveller

2
A design
B totals
C square
D magic

3
A all
B any
C some
D nine

4
A constant
B average
C answer
D result

5
A odd
B other
C *lo-shu*
D remaining

6
A past
B departed
C passed
D transferred

7
A fun
B evil
C foreign
D magical

8
A sport
B religion
C pastime
D frustration

Class letter

Dear Class 6H

Thank you for your recent inquiry. May I take this opportunity to wish you all a very successful 2023. We all know how important Year 6 is in your schooling.

Next year you will be progressing to high school and it is important to have a solid understanding of the type of work you can **1** _____ in Term 1, 2024.

No doubt you will be pleased to know we will be dispatching your English text books within two weeks so you will have them for the school holidays. Your teacher tells me you have an **2** _____ based upon one of the more difficult passages.

Academic Book Publishing also produces a number of other **3** _____ containing comprehension exercises based **4** _____ works by present-day writers. These include *Staying Alive in Year Five* by John Marsden, *Undone* by Paul Jennings and *The Enemy You Killed* by Peter McFarlane. **5** _____ you require any of these works, ask your parents to fill in the blue **6** _____ form and enclose it with a cheque or credit-card details in the stamped, addressed envelope and return it to us. Orders received before the end of the month will be entitled to a 10% discount.

7 _____ you decide to purchase all five books in our present Modem Literature series, you will receive, free of charge, a student's diary **8** _____ in gold with the initials of your choice. Make sure you record the initials you wish to have on the diary.

May you have a very satisfying year. Academic Book Publications wishes you every success in your studies.

Yours sincerely

Carolyne Hurst, Marketing Division

For questions 1 to 8, choose the answer which best fits the meaning and style of the passage.

1
A try
B expect
C manage
D purchase

2
A test
B project
C contract
D assignment

3
A texts
B shops
C schools
D worksheets

4
A in
B by
C on
D about

5
A After
B Would
C Should
D Before

6
A pay
B order
C address
D envelope

7
A If
B As
C When
D Although

8
A drawn
B carved
C sprayed
D embossed

MINI TEST 17: Narrative

15 MIN

The dead of the night

In one of those crazy moments of intuition I realised how much Lee wanted us to make this attack; if tanks had been rolling straight at us I don't think he would have moved. He was very into honour and revenge.

Homer looked calmer but he hadn't spoken. He had a bottle in each hand.

I could hear the **1** _____ now; the leading ones were dropping a gear, so we were probably close to the cutting. I grabbed my bottles and fished out my cigarette lighter. The dull headlights of the first truck were starting to show **2** _____ the trees. The convoys always had their headlights covered by some stuff that kept the light down to a **3** _____ glow. I guess they were scared of air attacks, but we didn't see too many of our planes these days, so I'd say **4** _____ drivers felt pretty safe.

We were hoping to change that.

Now the straining engines relaxed; there were several quick gear changes and the trucks started to roll, gathering speed through the **5** _____. We had placed ourselves on a bank so that as they came out of the cutting we'd be above them on the curve. We reckoned they would be travelling fast, easing across the road towards us as they **6** _____ the bend. And we were right. They sure did accelerate. They seemed to be there in an instant. The roar of the engines was suddenly coming straight at **7** _____, unobstructed by any more trees or banks. I had a good **8** _____ of the first three, all of them trucks, dark green in colour, tray tops with gates and tarps.

Then everything went wild. The first truck seemed to blow both its front tyres at the same moment. It was like a bomb going off. There was an almighty explosion. I couldn't believe how loud it was, nor how much smoke. Bits of rubber, **9** _____ of rubber went shredding across the road .

The truck slid straight across the road at high speed, back tyres screaming, and slammed against a tree.

By John Marsden

For questions 1 to 9, choose the answer which best fits the meaning and style of the passage.

1
A tanks
B trucks
C enemy
D soldiers

2
A up
B in
C past
D through

3
A soft
B bright
C useless
D sinister

4
A any
B some
C their
D there

5
A forest
B convoy
C tunnel
D cutting

6
A saw
B past
C left
D entered

7
A us
B me
C Lee
D them

8
A view
B look
C idea
D position

9
A lumps
B strips
C scraps
D clouds

10 MIN

There are three main written types:

- **The recognition of words that are incorrectly spelt**
  Exercises may look like this:
  For questions 1 and 2, choose the word that is incorrectly spelt. If there is no mistake, choose option **D**.

  1   A   alteration   **2**   A   bread

  B   territories   B   beard

  C   ponys   C   bared

  D   all correct   D   all correct

  The correct option is **C**.   The correct option is **D**.
  (The correct spelling is ponies.)   All words are correct.

- **The recognition of correct spelling in sentences**
  This is a little harder because a word on its own may be spelt correctly but in the context of a sentence could be incorrect. A common example is the misuse of 'their' and 'there'.
  Exercises may look like this:
  For question 1, choose the option in which there are **no** errors.

  1   A When I get home Mum's planning hour holiday arrangements.
         B When I get home Mums' planing our holiday arrangements.
         C When I get home Mum's planning our holiday arrangements.
         D When I get home Mums planning hour holiday arangements.

  The correct option is **C**.

  The mistakes are: **A** hour   **B** Mums', planing   **D** Mums, hour, arangements

- **The recognition of incorrectly spelt words in passages**
  The following type of exercise is less common, probably because it is more complex to mark. It is also a better test of your spelling. You are given a passage and are expected to recognise the incorrect word and then be able to spell it correctly. On the left-hand side of the passage, tick (✓) the line if there are no mistakes or put a cross (✗) if you find a mistake. Underline the incorrect word. Then correct the mistake in the space on the right-hand side of the passage. This is a form of editing.

  ✓   Although the internet is one of the most talked about things around,   _____

  ✗   most of the population <u>do'nt</u> understand it. Most people may need   _____ *don't*

  ✗   a 'guided tour'. <u>Physicaly</u> the internet is a vast number of computers,   _____ *Physically*

  ✗   of all sizes and types, connected through a variety of <u>circiuts</u> such   _____ *circuits*

  ✓   as high-capacity optical-fibre 'backbones'.   _____

  On the following pages there are some spelling tests of all three types.

For each question, choose the word that is incorrectly spelt. If there is no mistake, choose option **D**.

Mini Test 1

1
A radios
B pianos
C tomatoes
D all correct

2
A revolt
B rebell
C avenge
D all correct

3
A brake
B clutch
C accelerater
D all correct

4
A doubly
B crescent
C editer
D all correct

5
A annuall
B rotation
C eclipse
D all correct

6
A lettuce
B cucumber
C pumpken
D all correct

7
A reddest
B midday
C unnamed
D all correct

8
A submit
B frightning
C experiment
D all correct

9
A printers
B copiers
C duplicaters
D all correct

10
A cinnamon
B choral
C delta
D all correct

Mini Test 2

1
A spirit
B sprite
C spied
D all correct

2
A ghost
B ghastly
C ghoul
D all correct

3
A ginger
B pepper
C garlick
D all correct

4
A funell
B spout
C bucket
D all correct

5
A ancient
B antique
C original
D all correct

6
A infectious
B imfamous
C unfounded
D all correct

7
A houseing
B chimney
C residence
D all correct

8
A juicy
B mellon
C squash
D all correct

9
A it's
B its'
C its
D all correct

10
A caffeine
B cholesterol
C chord
D all correct

8 min

For each question, choose the word that is incorrectly spelt. If there is no mistake, choose option **D**.

Mini Test 3

1
A diet
B hicup
C plaster
D all correct

2
A kerocene
B microbe
C speedometer
D all correct

3
A miniature
B among
C aweful
D all correct

4
A written
B banjos
C develope
D all correct

5
A aquarium
B arches
C addresses
D all correct

6
A crazily
B fantasy
C busses
D all correct

7
A cargoes
B classic
C coconut
D all correct

8
A guitar
B frequent
C gnawed
D all correct

9
A pulleys
B octapus
C quarrel
D all correct

10
A can't
B wont
C you'll
D all correct

Mini Test 4

1
A bycycle
B trident
C ambulance
D all correct

2
A superior
B awkwordly
C essential
D all correct

3
A unusuall
B radiation
C collapsing
D all correct

4
A multiple
B divisor
C additionally
D all correct

5
A publically
B critically
C privately
D all correct

6
A scratchy
B screech
C scrounge
D all correct

7
A livelihood
B occupation
C proffession
D all correct

8
A grateful
B glazier
C greenery
D all correct

9
A cache
B robberies
C cheif
D all correct

10
A bunyip
B gargoyle
C hydra
D all correct

8 MIN

For each question, choose the word that is incorrectly spelt. If there is no mistake, choose option **D**.

Mini Test 5

1
A Britain
B Antartica
C Indonesia
D all correct

2
A topaz
B diamond
C emerald
D all correct

3
A helm
B keel
C cabbin
D all correct

4
A wierd
B twisted
C foreboding
D all correct

5
A canoe
B clipper
C hydrafoil
D all correct

6
A truant
B hostage
C ancestor
D all correct

7
A patron
B pattern
C patent
D all correct

8
A dwindel
B dynamite
C dux
D all correct

9
A dwelling
B dawdle
C dutifull
D all correct

10
A monstrosity
B orbital
C although
D all correct

Mini Test 6

1
A loosen
B paste
C pasta
D all correct

2
A purerly
B deceive
C revive
D all correct

3
A falcon
B appeal
C permit
D all correct

4
A altar
B aisle
C pew
D all correct

5
A wheather
B airy
C cyclone
D all correct

6
A obedient
B artful
C surley
D all correct

7
A cordial
B syrup
C essense
D all correct

8
A terrace
B foyar
C patio
D all correct

9
A rebuke
B stunted
C marvel
D all correct

10
A contenental
B strives
C brasserie
D all correct

For each question, choose the word that is incorrectly spelt. If there is no mistake, choose option **D**.

Mini Test 7

1
A leveling
B corner
C landscape
D all correct

2
A tobacco
B solos
C submitt
D all correct

3
A quarrelled
B yourselves
C seperate
D all correct

4
A basicly
B zeros
C rare
D all correct

5
A proofs
B potatos
C shyly
D all correct

6
A guaranteed
B fastened
C debit
D all correct

7
A fanciful
B rotation
C moterist
D all correct

8
A incorrect
B mispelt
C wrong
D all correct

9
A imature
B insecure
C conscious
D all correct

10
A Indian
B Pacific
C Atlandic
D all correct

Mini Test 8

1
A commandor
B concise
C eagerly
D all correct

2
A embattled
B personall
C embedded
D all correct

3
A infinitive
B superstructure
C iregular
D all correct

4
A differing
B abdomon
C technical
D all correct

5
A circuits
B modems
C snippets
D all correct

6
A tonne
B billed
C incentive
D all correct

7
A illusionist
B crippling
C modles
D all correct

8
A alocate
B periodically
C bracelets
D all correct

9
A browse
B nibble
C gargle
D all correct

10
A functions
B jest
C gala
D all correct

For each question, choose the word that is incorrectly spelt. If there is no mistake, choose option **D**.

Mini Test 9

1
A slobbered
B complication
C shun
D all correct

2
A Adelaide
B Darwin
C Melborne
D all correct

3
A fasting
B uncomfortable
C indulging
D all correct

4
A crass
B hyphen
C wherever
D all correct

5
A coarse
B proposition
C preposition
D all correct

6
A apostrophe
B shortened
C contration
D all correct

7
A hiaku
B elderly
C detailing
D all correct

8
A auditions
B hydrogen
C bangals
D all correct

9
A circumstants
B teething
C fortieth
D all correct

10
A hysterical
B latatude
C mason
D all correct

Mini Test 10

1
A gravell
B happily
C detonate
D all correct

2
A colonies
B donkeys
C subsidies
D all correct

3
A sever
B embark
C beneficial
D all correct

4
A attatch
B uselessness
C witches
D all correct

5
A safety
B talons
C dangrous
D all correct

6
A preening
B regulater
C screeching
D all correct

7
A noxious
B connexion
C fingerling
D all correct

8
A cuaseway
B cannibal
C ointment
D all correct

9
A aford
B atrocious
C cannery
D all correct

10
A velvety
B furyious
C cabaret
D all correct

For each question, choose the word that is incorrectly spelt. If there is no mistake, choose option **D**.

Mini Test 11

1
A wintry
B summery
C nursery
D all correct

2
A springy
B February
C bouncey
D all correct

3
A prior
B meddley
C taxis
D all correct

4
A coccoon
B receipt
C religious
D all correct

5
A insecticide
B savagery
C ageing
D all correct

6
A usefulness
B tongues
C ewes
D all correct

7
A anchor
B yellowing
C drunkeness
D all correct

8
A sincerly
B putrid
C camouflage
D all correct

9
A quay
B perescope
C monastery
D all correct

10
A commonwealth
B democracy
C fedarel
D all correct

Mini Test 12

1
A sizable
B trumpetter
C turquoise
D all correct

2
A ellect
B ordinary
C happiness
D all correct

3
A sheriff
B sapphire
C wreath
D all correct

4
A gnarled
B adjoin
C glucose
D all correct

5
A rapture
B rupture
C rupee
D all correct

6
A glycerine
B buzard
C adolescent
D all correct

7
A hazzard
B cubic
C awe
D all correct

8
A imp
B hotelier
C combersome
D all correct

9
A fasinate
B laminate
C detention
D all correct

10
A ambassador
B laughing
C monopolly
D all correct

MINI TEST 1: Finding errors

For each question, choose the option in which there are **no** errors.

1 A Working closely with the motorest the mechanic was able to repair the generarter.
   B Working closely with the motorist the mechanic was able to repair the generater.
   C Working closely with the motorist the mechanic was able to repair the generator.
   D Working closely with the motorest the mechanic was able to repare the generator.

2 A A selection of fine tropical fruit was presented to the foreign guests.
   B A selection of fine tropical friut was presented to the foriegn guests.
   C A selection of fine tropical fruit was precented too the foreign guests.
   D A selection of fine tropical fruit was presented too the foreign guestes.

3 A Doctors used to think that people who walked in their sleep where acting out their dreams.
   B Doctors use to think that people who walked in there sleep were acting out there dreams.
   C Doctors used to think that people who walked in their sleep were acting out their dreams.
   D Doctors use to think that poeple who walked in their sleep were acting out their dreams.

4 A Jealousy, resentfullness and suspicion are some of the emotions of those who feel betrayed.
   B Jelousy, resentfulness and suspicion are some of the emotions of those who feal betrayed.
   C Jealousy, resentfulness and suspicion are some of the emotions of those who feel betrayed.
   D Jealousy, resentfullness and suspicion are some off the emotions of those who feel betrayed.

5 A The steamer witch carried one hundred and forty passengers sliped out of the harbour.
   B The steamer which carried one hundred and forty passengers slipped out of the harbour.
   C The steamor which carried one hundred and forety passengers sliped out of the harbour.
   D The steamer which carryed one hundred and fourty passengers slipped out of the harbour.

For each question, choose the option in which there are **no** errors.

1.
  A Suddenly Gary burst from the garage tearing at he's jacket.
  B Suddenly Gary burst from the garage tearing at his jacket.
  C Suddenly Gary burst from the garage tareing at his jackett.
  D Suddenly Gary burst from the garage tearing at hes jacket.

2.
  A The satellite was caterpulted from a orbit around Venus into an endless journey to outer space.
  B The sattelite was catapulted from an orbet around Venus into an endless journey to outer space.
  C The satallite was caterpulted from a orbit around Venus into an endless journey to outer space.
  D The satellite was catapulted from an orbit around Venus into an endless journey to outer space.

3.
  A "The grass is too wet to sit on," exclaimed the instructor, "there's been a heavy dew."
  B "The grass is too wet to sit on," exclamed the instructor. "there's been a heavy dew."
  C "The grass is to wet too sit on," exclaimed the instructer, "theres been a heavy dew."
  D "The grass is to wet to sit on," exclaimed the instructor. "their's been a heavy due."

4.
  A She closed her eyes relucdently. I was surprised the arguement hadn't continued further.
  B She closed her eyes relucdently. I was surprized the arguement had'nt continued further.
  C She closed her eyes reluctantly. I was surprized the argument hadn't continued further.
  D She closed her eyes reluctantly. I was surprised the argument hadn't continued further.

5.
  A Halfway down the ally Elaines manner changed. She became wary, nervous and quite.
  B Halfway down the ally Elaines manner changed. She became warey, nervous and quite.
  C Halfway down the alley Elaine's manner changed .She became wary, nervous and quiet.
  D Halfway down the ally Elaines' maner changed . She became warry, nervous and quiet.

For each question, choose the option in which there are **no** errors.

1 A The cheif inspector was waiting to rebuke him for murmurring while being questioned.
  B The chief inspector was waiting to rebuke him for murmuring while being questioned.
  C The chief inspecter was waiting too rebuke him for murmuring while being questioned.
  D The cheif inspector was waiting to rebuke him for murmuring while being questioned.

2 A Once confronted by the somber reality of the obstacle itself, Trudy collected her thoughts.
  B Once confronted by the sombre reallity of the obstacle itself, Trudy collected her thoughs.
  C Once confrounted by the somber reality of the obsticle itself, Trudy collected her thoughts.
  D Once confronted by the sombre reality of the obstacle itself, Trudy collected her thoughts.

3 A A nearby clump of bamboo shivered and parted and there it was, huge in the enclosing mist.
  B A nearby clump of bamboo shivvered and parted and their it was, huge in the encloseing mist.
  C A nearby clump of bamboo shivered and parted and there it was, huge in the encloseing mist.
  D A nereby clump of bamboo shivered and parted and there it was, huge in the enclosing missed.

4 A While renching at the car door Debby lossed her hat, which was flattened by parsing traffic.
  B While wrenching at the car door Debby lost her hat, which was flattened by passing traffic.
  C While wrenching at the car door Debby lost her hat, which was flatened by passing traffic.
  D While renching at the car door Debby lost her hat, which was flatened by passing traffic.

5 A Here the author has spun an intriguing tale of haunting fantasy set in the western dessert.
  B Hear the author has spun an intreguing tale of haunting fantasy set in the westen desert.
  C Hear the author has spun an intreguing tail of haunting fantasy set in the western desert.
  D Here the author has spun an intriguing tale of haunting fantasy set in the western desert.

MINI TEST 4: Finding errors

10 MIN

For each question, choose the option in which there are **no** errors.

1
A Depositting cheques on a Saturday is good for customer relation's as well as improving profits.
B Depositing cheques on a Saturday is good for customer relations as well as improveing profits.
C Depositing cheques on a Saturday is good for customer relations as well as improving profits.
D Depositting checks on a Saturday is good for customer relations as well as improving prophets.

2
A Baring his hairy chest before the audeince the wrestler roared defiantely at the promoter.
B Baring his hairy chest before the audience the wrestler roared defiantly at the promoter.
C Barring his hairy chest before the audience the wrestler roared defiantely at the promotor.
D Barring his hairy chest before the audience the wrestler roared defiantly at the premotor.

3
A Where is the book that explains grammar rules which students can then put into practice?
B Where is the book that explains grammer rules which students can than put into practice?
C Where is the book that explanes grammer rules which students can then put into practise?
D Where is the book that explains grammar rules which student's can then put into practise?

4
A Kelly did not concentrait on her lessons as she was more concerned about the enviroment.
B Kelly did not concentrate on her lessons as she was more concernd about the environment.
C Kelly did not concentrate on her lessens as she was more concerned about the enviroment.
D Kelly did not concentrate on her lessons as she was more concerned about the environment.

5
A Appalled at being horse during the rehearsel Sally looked for a suitable medicine.
B Appauled at being hoarse during the rehearsal Sally looked for a suitable medicene.
C Appalled at being hoarse during the rehearsal Sally looked for a suitable medicine.
D Appaled at being hoarse during the rehearsel Sally looked for a suitable medicine.

For each question, choose the option in which there are **no** errors.

1 A Sundry items were found lying on the front lawn after the party.
    B Sundery items were found lieing on the frount lawn after the party.
    C Sundry items we're found lying on the front lawn after the party.
    D Sundery items where found lyeing on the front lawn after the party.

2 A Whenever there is moisture in the air I get an asthma attack.
    B Whenever there is moisteur in the air I get an ashma attack.
    C Whenever their's moisture in the air I get a asthma attack.
    D Whenever their is moisture in the air I get an ashma attack.

3 A We tiptoed form the office and went back to the waiting room to reed magazines.
    B We tiptoed from the office and went back to the waiting room to reed magazines.
    C We tiptoed from the office and whent back to the waiting room to read magazenes.
    D We tiptoed from the office and went back to the waiting room to read magazines.

4 A The buzzer was going and we had Swiming which was one of my favourite sports.
    B The buzzer was going and we had Swimming which was one of my favourite sports.
    C The buzzer was going and we had Swiming which was one of my favorite sports.
    D The buzzer was goeing and we had Swimming witch was one of my favourite sports.

5 A Helicopters, gliders and other fixed winged aircraft were destroyed in the tornadoes.
    B Helicoptors, gliders and other fixed winged aercraft were destroyed in the tornadoes.
    C Helicopters, gliders and other fixed winged aircraft where destroyed in the tornados.
    D Helicoptors, gliders and other fixed winged aercraft where destroyed in the tornados.

For each question, choose the option in which there are **no** errors.

1 **A** A separate sheet, written by the applicant, should be attached to performance experience.
   B A seperate sheet, writen by the applicant, should be attached to performance experience.
   C A separate sheet, writen by the applicant, should be attached to proformance experience.
   D A seperate sheet, written by the applicant, should be attached to performance expereince.

2 **A** He wondered idoly where you discovered humorous storys to whisper too girls.
   B He wandered idly where you discovered humorous stories to whisper to girls.
   C He wondered idley where you descovered humorous storeys to whisper to girls.
   D He wondered idly where you discovered humorous stories to whisper to girls.

3 **A** From the cellar they heard the telephone ring in the redecorated lounge room.
   B From the cellar they heard the telephone ring in the redecarated longe room.
   C From the celler they herd the telephone ring in the redecorated lounge room.
   D Form the celler they heard the telephone ring in the redecorated lounge room.

4 **A** Two suvivers of a shipwreck shelter in a cave knowing they will not be rescued.
   B Two survivors of a shipreck shelter in a cave nowing they will not be rescured.
   C Two survivors of a shipwreck shelter in a cave knowing they will not be rescued.
   D Two survivors of a shipwreck shelter in a cave knowing they will not be resued.

5 **A** The site forman was in charge of issuing jobs on a first come, first served basis.
   B The site foreman was in charge of issueing jobs on a first come, first served basis.
   C The site foreman was in charge of issuing jobs on a first come, first served basis.
   D The site forman was in charge of issuing jobs on a first come, first served bases.

For each question, choose the option in which there are **no** errors.

1 **A** It's easyer to call London but you must do it by midday.
   B It's easier to call London but you must do it by midday.
   C Its easier to call London but you must do it by miday.
   D Its easier to call London but you must do it by midday.

2 **A** Meat the people who have taken out the award fore story writting.
   B Met the people who have takken out the award for story writing.
   C Meet the peopel who have takken out the award fore story writting.
   D Meet the people who have taken out the award for story writing.

3 **A** The leader of the skiing team was hoping for a fast run down the western slope.
   B The leader of the sking team was hopeing for a fast run down the westen slope.
   C The leader of the skiing teem was hopping for a fast run down the western slope.
   D The leader of the sking team was hoping for a fast run down the westen slope.

4 **A** The berth of a tiny possum in the ceiling upset our parents.
   B The berth of a tinny possum in the cieling upset our parents.
   C The birth of a tiny possum in the ceiling upset our parents.
   D The birth of a tinny possum in the cieling upset our parents.

5 **A** Molly bought me an expensive canary in a golden cage for my birthday.
   B Molly bought me an expensive cannary in a goldern cage for my birthday.
   C Molly brought me an expensive canary in a goldern cage for my birthday.
   D Molly brought me an expensive cannary in a golden cage for my berthday.

12 min

For each question, choose the option in which there are **no** errors.

1　**A** "Innocent? Its not a word I'd expect a criminal like you to say," bawled the detective.
　　B "Innocent? Its not a word I'd expect a criminal like you to say," bowled the detective.
　　C "Innosent? It's not a word I'd exspect a criminal like you to say," bawled the detective.
　　D "Innocent? It's not a word I'd expect a criminal like you to say," bawled the detective.

2　**A** When the cannons on the ships were fired the villages came out into the street.
　　B When the cannons on the ships were fired the villagers came out into the street.
　　C When the canons on the ships were fired the villagies came our into the street.
　　D When the canons on the ships were fired the villagers came out into the street.

3　**A** The skies were firy red as the sun set.
　　B The skys were fiery red as the sun set.
　　C The skies were firey red as the son set.
　　D The skies were fiery red as the sun set.

4　**A** The mudy water was too foul for domestic use.
　　B The muddy warter was to foul for domestic use.
　　C The muddy water was too foul for domestic use.
　　D The mudy water was to fowl for domestic use.

5　**A** The girls lead their dogs across the parade grounds every evening.
　　B The gril's lead their dogs accross the parade grounds every evening.
　　C The girls led their dogs across the parade grounds every evenning.
　　D The girl's led there dogs accross the parade grounds every evening.

On the left-hand side of the passage, tick (✔) the line if there are no mistakes or put a cross (✗) if you find a mistake. Underline the incorrect word. Correct the mistake in the space on the right-hand side of the passage.

1 A _____ I take the signed note back to the Principle. I'm off to the Gold Coast _____

B _____ and I'm going as fast as I can to get out of this place, but I feel like a _____

C _____ traitor. My best friend will think I'm as inconsiderate as the worsed _____

D _____ kids in the school are. Holly will think I'm an idieot going to another _____

E _____ state but Dad has to go. Mum wants to go and I am not staying in this _____

F _____ cold-in-winter, hot-in-summer prision any longer. _____

2 A _____ Toby didn't answer me. He's allways like that first thing in the _____

B _____ morning. Silent, brouding and clumsy. Dad says it's best to leave him _____

C _____ alone. He calls him a late starter. Mum says his more like a slow _____

D _____ starter. Personly I like to think of him as awkward—or maybe it's _____

E _____ a trick too get out of helping with the breakfast and the washing up. _____

F _____ Mum never asks him to help anymore. She just rolls her eyes. _____

3 A _____ Miss Gray is our geography teacher. What dose a geography teacher _____

B _____ do? Whatever it is, she loves it. She collects globes, and atlasses and _____

C _____ cracked maps that have spent much of their time rolled up on top of _____

D _____ the cupbord. She gets really excited when someone asks a question _____

E _____ about some strange place—and she probably went their on her last _____

F _____ holidays. Then next day we get all her personal photographs! _____

4 A _____ Luke settled down with the chocolates and Coke. He knew how to _____

B _____ prepare himself befor the feature film began. Almost from the first _____

C _____ moment I was in some state of agany or fear. I forgot about the food _____

D _____ completely and hung onto the the arm rests as if I was in a dentist's _____

E _____ chair. When the bombs exploded I flinched, stiffled a scream and _____

F _____ even ducked for pretection in one realistic battle scene. _____

On the left-hand side of the passage, tick (✔) the line if there are no mistakes or put a cross (✗) if you find a mistake. Underline the incorrect word. Correct the mistake in the space on the right-hand side of the passage.

1 A _____ The ball came tumbling towards Josh, bouncing over the tuffs of   _____

    B _____ grass. He could imagine himself trapping it and kicking it back   _____

    C _____ across the field towards the gaol posts. Then somehow he was   _____

    D _____ stareing at the spectators again and the ball had gone past. A parent   _____

    E _____ had to run and fetch it. Josh began to feel miserable. Suddenly he   _____

    F _____ found the hole game extremely silly and boring.   _____

2 A _____ It was then I sneaked away, up a side staircase and back to the   _____

    B _____ gallerey. The roof was ancient cedar beams and though the floor was   _____

    C _____ rough now, people had entertained there in passed centuries. Sunlight   _____

    D _____ shone on the floor making geometric paterns from the diamond   _____

    E _____ pains of the leadlight windows. I blinked rapidly to get used to the   _____

    F _____ brightness after the gloom of the stairs. Where to now? Home?   _____

3 A _____ The National Libary for the Handicapped Child was established   _____

    B _____ in 1985 to help those who care for children who's handicap affects   _____

    C _____ their ability to read. In 1988 it was given an award for outstanding   _____

    D _____ servises to children and books. They offer a wide range of   _____

    E _____ selected books which are interesting and suitable for children having   _____

    F _____ difficulties in reading what is currantly available to them.   _____

4 A _____ Mr Smith was of English descent, a tall, handsom man of about forty,   _____

    B _____ with a very correct, militery bearing. He was employed by a bank to   _____

    C _____ act as a security gaurd. One day a beggar told Mr Smith that he had   _____

    D _____ been in the army with him. Mr Smith tried to ignor him but was curious   _____

    E _____ for the man spoke excelent English. Although he never gave money to   _____

    F _____ beggars he was never unfriendly. He pretended to remain aloof.   _____

MINI TEST 1: Alphabetical order

The next tests are based on your undersanding of alphabetical order.

For each question, choose the option according to alphabetical order.

1 Which word comes after **fatal**?
A fare
B fatty
C fasten
D after

2 Which word comes after **aerodrome**?
A aeroplane
B about
C abbot
D aerial

3 Which word comes after **eel**?
A east
B effect
C elect
D dealer

4 Which word comes after **couplet**?
A couples
B coop
C coupon
D droplet

5 Which word comes after **czar**?
A damsel
B crazy
C dazzle
D daze

6 Which word comes after **school**?
A scholar
B sacred
C secret
D schooner

7 Which word comes after **trick**?
A tricky
B trickle
C track
D truck

8 Which word comes after **warrant**?
A war
B warranty
C warren
D warrior

9 Which word comes after **zigzag**?
A zebra
B zipper
C zenith
D zero

For each question, choose the option according to alphabetical order.

1 Which word comes before **iceman**?
A icy
B ice
C icing
D icicle

2 Which word comes before **prosecutor**?
A prosperity
B prospector
C proscribe
D prosperous

3 Which word comes before **meadow**?
A mead
B meantime
C meal
D meander

4 Which word comes before **Auckland**?
A Austin
B Auburn
C Austria
D Australia

5 Which word comes before **secrecy**?
A secure
B secret
C section
D second

6 Which word comes before **nutmeg**?
A nursery
B nylons
C nutrition
D nuts

7 Which word comes before **dress**?
A dressing
B dresser
C drench
D dressmaker

8 Which word comes before **shadow**?
A shearer
B shape
C shambles
D shadiness

9 Which word comes before **hunger**?
A humorous
B husband
C hunter
D hurdle

For each question, choose the option according to alphabetical order.

1 Which word comes after **elastic**?
  A erratic
  B escape
  C effect
  D essay

2 Which word comes after **doomsday**?
  A dormouse
  B doorman
  C drool
  D doorpost

3 Which word comes after **grunt**?
  A graze
  B grapes
  C going
  D hauty

4 Which word comes after **Woolloomooloo**?
  A Wollombi
  B Woollahra
  C Woolloongabba
  D Wollstoncraft

5 Which word comes after **yes**?
  A yesterday
  B yern
  C yet
  D yellow

6 Which word comes after **window**?
  A wince
  B widow
  C width
  D winner

7 Which word comes after **question**?
  A quest
  B questionnaire
  C queue
  D quiche

8 Which word comes after **invisible**?
  A invoice
  B involve
  C invoke
  D involvement

9 Which word comes after **crook**?
  A crocodile
  B cropping
  C croon
  D crooked

Vocabulary exercises are designed to test how well you understand words, especially how they are used in written and spoken language. Vocabulary questions can arise in comprehension tests, cloze tests and editing exercises. Tests of vocabulary include questions in a variety of forms.

Example 1: Choose the option that is **closest** in meaning (i.e. a synonym) to the word in **bold**.

They talked about the **odd** weather they were having that summer.

A uneven

B strange

C changeable

D unpredictable   The best answer is **B**.

Example 2: Choose the option that has the **opposite** meaning (i.e. an antonym) to the word in **bold.**

Trudy was an imaginative and **efficient** cook.   It was an **outdated** journal full of strange facts.

A flamboyant	A	fashionable
B productive	B	antiquated
C inefficient	C	useful
D misuse	D	rare

The best answer is C.   The best answer is A.

Example 3: Read the sentence below and choose the best answer for the question.

The painting was finished with **bold** brush strokes.

In which sentence does **bold** have the same meaning?

A Kevin was a bold little boy and upset many adults.

B Her final school report had all the poor results in bold print.

C Using bold designs and flashy materials, her sports wear became very trendy.

D When playing Monopoly a bold move might be to buy hotels as quickly as possible.

The best answer is C.

Example 4: Choose the option that best explains the word in **bold**.

The principal always **digressed** toward the end of his talks in assembly.

A ensured all students listened

B departed from the topic

C hurried off

D got excited   The best answer is **B**.

Example 5: Choose the word (or phrase) that best completes the sentence.

We raced for the train _____ there was another one at 9:05.

A so

B because

C although

D therefore   The best answer is **C**.

Example 6: Choose the word that would be **least** appropriate when describing a delay.

A late

B detained

C frustration

D breakfast   The least appropriate word would be option **D**.

MINI TEST 1: Synonyms

For each question, choose the option closest in meaning or most similar to (i.e. a synonym of) the word(s) in **bold**.

■

1 They talked about the **mild** weather they were enjoying for November.
A calm
B weak
C gentle
D pleasant

2 After breakfast he **lounged** in front of the television feeling good.
A waited
B dozed
C lazed
D sat

3 An old man was kneeling on the lawn, **vigorously** pulling out weeds from a side garden bed.
A eagerly
B carefully
C strenuously
D energetically

4 They made quite an uproar for such a small **gathering**.
A group
B collection
C audience
D celebration

5 It didn't take long to deliver the notices and **draw up** the petition sheets.
A design
B collect
C illustrate
D withdraw

6 Nikki **gritted** her teeth and began to look straight ahead.
A cleaned
B clenched
C clicked
D closed

7 Holly left the house for school and **braced** herself for the stares and whispers.
A steadied
B fastened
C organised
D calmed

8 Jamie's mother was at the **head** of the parade as it went down Wentworth St.
A top
B front
C start
D crown

9 Many animals visit this **haunt** for food and water.
A forest
B frighten
C location
D rendezvous

For each question, choose the option closest in meaning or most similar to (i.e. a synonym of) the word(s) in **bold**.

1 A **lean** dog could be seen near the far shed.
A thin
B pitiful
C resting
D prowling

2 Carnivorous plants have strange **ruses** to attract and trap their prey.
A tricks
B colours
C inventions
D adaptations

3 Once we have made our decisions we should not **deviate** from those set plans of action.
A look
B turn
C march
D be released

4 The engineers, fearing road congestion, wanted to **curb** the flow of traffic into the city.
A examine
B restrict
C slow
D stop

5 Because they were expecting an attack the pirates began **hoarding** weapons.
A accumulating
B looking for
C loading
D saving

6 After the argument with her parents Kim became very **subdued**.
A angry
B sorry
C quiet
D depressed

7 The information in the science textbook was not only poorly presented but obviously **dated**.
A obsolete
B labelled
C incorrect
D ancient

8 The explorer, Captain Scott, did not make much **headway** during the blizzard.
A room
B coverage
C progress
D improvement

9 The netball players worked out a new **manoeuvre** for the final in Round 1.
A tactic
B dodge
C exercise
D challenge

For each question, choose the option closest in meaning or most similar to (i.e. a synonym of) the word(s) in **bold**.

1 Surveyors **fought** their way through jungle-covered gorges.
A brawled
B defended
C struggled
D grappled

2 Sadler's new novel **provokes** some interesting ideas about women in the armed services.
A develops
B conceals
C provides
D raises

3 Please do not leave the room in that **manner** again.
A way
B mood
C hurry
D direction

4 All school accounts must be paid **prior** to the first day of term so that enrolments can be finalised.
A on
B after
C before
D during

5 When you **meddle in** their plans all you do is upset the camp organisers.
A ignore
B assist with
C argue about
D interfere with

6 Father wanted to **negotiate** a sale price for his old car but the buyer was not interested.
A offer
B demand
C work out
D pass through

7 When the moon is in this **phase** of its cycle I always expect we will get some rain.
A fade
B stage
C section
D fraction

8 It will be a **pointless** trip if we cannot bring home some samples.
A blunt
B absurd
C scoreless
D meaningless

9 *The Famous Five* was a **popular** book when my parents were at school.
A cheap
B common
C well-liked
D widespread

For each question, choose the option closest in meaning or most similar to (i.e. a synonym of) the word(s) in **bold**.

1 Just imagine a huge **shimmering** curtain of light across the night sky!
 A glaring
 B colourful
 C glistening
 D unsteady

2 It takes **practice** to fly a kite really well.
 A skill
 B patience
 C many tries
 D endurance

3 His **apparel** was in tatters after the trek through the forest.
 A suit
 B apron
 C clothing
 D appearance

4 The old sea chest was **cast** onto the sandy beach by the rolling surf.
 A rolled
 B thrown
 C floated
 D pounded

5 There was a silent wait while the men watched the hounds **questing** for a scent.
 A sniffing
 B searching
 C exploring
 D journeying

6 There was still a **band** of archers that held their ground among the burning buildings.
 A group
 B crowd
 C regiment
 D collection

7 The prisoner **evidently** understood the question but refused to answer.
 A possibly
 B probably
 C apparently
 D should have

8 'At some **point** we should look for shelter,' said the guide.
 A dot
 B stop
 C stage
 D direct

9 Your **position** in the debate on endangered species was well argued.
 A posture
 B location
 C attitude
 D viewpoint

MINI TEST 5: Synonyms

For each question, choose the option closest in meaning or most similar to (i.e. a synonym of) the word(s) in **bold**.

1 For his size Justin was as **game** as any player.
A sporting
B daring
C quick
D fair

2 The police had **lavish** praise for the neighbour who saved the swimmers.
A open
B cautious
C luxurious
D abundant

3 The judge was **nettled** by comments he saw in the paper.
A teased
B angered
C irritated
D saddened

4 Marnie was a shy girl and her confident behaviour during the quest was all **show**.
A a trick
B pretence
C good fun
D entertainment

5 Some children in the class were rather **bold** when the visitor entered the room with a parrot.
A daring
B cheeky
C lively
D loud

6 The old farmer had an **inexplicable** understanding of weather changes.
A uncanny
B inspired
C ominous
D outstanding

7 The kitten was treated more as a **plaything** than a pet.
A toy
B hobby
C pastime
D distraction

8 One player **scoffed** at the coach's new plans for winning back the trophy.
A jeered at
B belittled
C condemned
D laughed at

9 The last goal caused a **tumultuous** roar from the supporters in the grandstand.
A raging
B stormy
C excited
D unrestrained

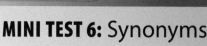

For each question, choose the option closest in meaning or most similar to (i.e. a synonym of) the word(s) in **bold**.

1 The young bears were **basking** in a small clearing in the forest.
A enjoying the warmth and light
B playing happily together
C cleaning their fur
D exploring for food

2 On the stage Anna appeared **ungainly** and badly costumed.
A to be making little progress
B slow and deliberate
C without support
D clumsy

3 The soldier **tottered** on the edge of the castle wall.
A crouched
B wobbled
C was drinking
D stood on tiptoes

4 That is your **opinion** and I don't want to know about it.
A judgement
B mistake
C belief
D fault

5 Even after returning from hospital my father was **sluggish**.
A overtired
B slipping over
C slow moving
D drooping more and more

6 Late in summer the town was **engulfed** by fire.
A taken over
B destroyed
C swallowed up
D encircled

7 The **distraught** parents were not allowed to join in the search for the children.
A easily upset
B very agitated
C sedated
D raving

8 Yvonne writes many songs and that was the most **melodious** one for a long time.
A tuneful
B catchy
C musical
D pleasing

9 It is claimed that the knights of the crusades were full of **valour** and dedication.
A power
B daring
C courage
D sincerity

MINI TEST 7: Synonyms

For each question, choose the option closest in meaning or most similar to (i.e. a synonym of) the word(s) in **bold**.

1 The exhibition was **drawing to a close** and the organisers felt very satisfied with their profits.
A creating interest
B attracting crowds
C bringing pleasure
D nearing the end

2 The store's regular offer of free lottery tickets was no more than a **gimmick**.
A gadget
B trick
C stunt
D joke

3 The medical officers moved **gingerly** across the broken glass.
A timidly
B silently
C cautiously
D suspiciously

4 All her life she had been worried by an **ongoing** back problem.
A unusual
B persistent
C painful
D annoying

5 The film showed a visitor about to **tender** money to the guard.
A slip
B offer
C deliver
D contribute

6 At the end of the year most students felt somewhat **indifferent** when the holiday courses were announced.
A aloof
B unmoved
C insulted
D interested

7 The visit to the abattoir left an **indelible** mark on their memories.
A faint
B cruel
C lasting
D temporary

8 Everyone in our street found Mel to be an **undisciplined** child.
A cheeky
B fearless
C uninvolved
D uncontrolled

9 A **fruitful** search through an antique store resulted in the purchase of two rocking chairs.
A worthwhile
B extensive
C fertile
D costly

10 MIN

For each question, choose the option closest in meaning or most similar to (i.e. a synonym of) the word(s) in **bold**.

1 After exploring the river for a suitable crossing I had to **concede** defeat.
A tolerate
B consider
C admit
D think about

2 As the soldier **scouted** the edge of the lake he discovered the tracks of another person.
A hiked
B searched
C surveyed
D patrolled

3 Mr Jones was **notorious** in the district for the loudness of his voice.
A famous
B unfavourably known
C respected
D little appreciated

4 The **noted** author stepped up to the lectern.
A popular
B articulate
C acclaimed
D prolific

5 The weather was **sultry** and building up to a storm.
A warm
B sullen
C refreshing
D stifling

6 My mother referred to the children **obliquely** as she spoke to the teacher.
A indirectly
B quietly
C carefully
D guiltily

7 At sixty-five years old Mr Burton had a **hankering** to return to the country in which he was born.
A need
B wish
C yearning
D expectation

8 Jake shuffled **dolefully** towards the Principal's office where his parents were waiting patiently.
A tiredly
B dismally
C painfully
D disinterestedly

9 According to my mother the bus driver's attitude was **downright** rude.
A clearly
B obviously
C thoroughly
D mistakenly

MINI TEST 9: Synonyms

For each question, choose the option closest in meaning or most similar to (i.e. a synonym of) the word(s) in **bold**.

1 Marianne did not appreciate the **tepid** bath after her two-day hike in the mountains.
A lukewarm
B shallow
C chilly
D dirty

2 Sudden movement in the back street **caught** her attention.
A attracted
B seized
C snared
D held

3 We were warned not to listen to **gossip**.
A idle talk
B rumours
C scandal
D lies

4 He wore a **gaudy** beach shirt to the school speech night.
A colourful and loose
B tasteless and showy
C bright and attractive
D unconventional and striking

5 Terri's older sister had to **keep** a diary when she went overseas.
A take care of
B maintain
C manage
D carry

6 The service station should **order** parts before the holidays.
A list
B demand
C send for
D apply for

7 The **onus** is on the policeperson to show that you had something to do with the broken window.
A hope
B obligation
C expectation
D opportunity

8 Acting **on impulse** the detective hurried to the back of the shed.
A foolishly
B recklessly
C on instructions
D without thought

9 We had another **scheme**: we would deliver the parcel ourselves.
A idea
B plan
C thought
D suggestion

MINI TEST 1: Antonyms

For each question, choose the option that has the **opposite** meaning (i.e. an antonym) to the word in **bold**.

1 She was a **qualified** plumber as soon as she finished her college studies.
A untrained
B thorough
C experienced
D incompetent

2 Paula's fingers were **numb** after making the snowman.
A dull
B hurting
C sensitive
D paralysed

3 Any **hasty** decision may be one we regret.
A slow
B sensible
C cautious
D delayed

4 Never use **transparent** wrapping paper on presents that are meant as a surprise.
A opaque
B bright
C recycled
D translucent

5 Some campers **observe** all the National Park regulations.
A obstruct
B disregard
C remember
D abide by

6 The weather in New York can be quite **severe**.
A mild
B soft
C gently
D forbidding

7 At his age grandfather can be **set** in his ways.
A free
B flexible
C undecided
D hardened

8 The critic **praised** the actor for continuing during the disturbance.
A mocked
B ignored
C enhanced
D condemned

9 Our school concert was a **disjointed** and rambling presentation.
A united
B rejoined
C confused
D cohesive

MINI TEST 2: Antonyms

For each question, choose the option that has the **opposite** meaning (i.e. an antonym) to the word in **bold**.

1 **Impartial** decisions are expected from all cricket umpires.
A honest
B biased
C correct
D supportive

2 Living in an **urban** area provides many people with the lifestyle they enjoy.
A rural
B lonely
C suburban
D populated

3 On inspecting the vases, the curator realised they were **originals**.
A copies
B frauds
C foreign
D old fashioned

4 The balloon began to **swell** as the day became hotter.
A wither
B inflate
C contract
D decrease

5 I **swear** that our team will play even better next match.
A disbelieve
B confirm
C refute
D lie

6 The teachers will **back** any plans the parents have for improving the grounds.
A resist
B favour
C finance
D undermine

7 To **ban** the use of chewing gum will upset many sportspeople.
A bar
B allow
C restrict
D encourage

8 Bindi's **eagerness** to participate in the swimming races impressed her team.
A zeal
B vagueness
C impatience
D indifference

9 The fruit was too **green** to be picked.
A ripe
B young
C deformed
D immature

MINI TEST 1: Words with multiple meanings

For each question, read the sentence and choose the best answer for each question.

1 The painting was finished with **fine** brush strokes.

In which sentence does **fine** have the same meaning?

A Grandmother used fine thread to complete the tapestry.

B The skies were clear and the weather was fine.

C Her final school report commended her on her fine work.

D In his dash for the bus he was cutting it fine.

2 If we **hole** the water container on the trip we may be in difficulties.

In which sentence does **hole** have the same meaning?

A The swimming hole was full of stagnant water.

B The hole in the fence was large enough to let the dog through.

C My father can hole a five metre put on the last green.

D To make sure we do not hole the petrol tank we will protect it with a steel plate.

3 The authorities will **discharge** water from the dams during droughts.

In which sentence does **discharge** have the same meaning?

A The discharge from her left eye required urgent treatment.

B To discharge a gun in a public place is against the law.

C The river will discharge factory waste into the sea if there is a flood.

D The captain will discharge the soldier for misconduct.

4 The fullback had a **spell** on the sidelines.

In which sentence does **spell** have the same meaning?

A A spell was cast over all the people in the castle.

B If you learn to spell, you will please your tutor.

C Spell it out for me in simple terms.

D During the hike the campers took a spell by the creek.

5 Before I **plot** my course on the map I need some advice.

In which sentence does **plot** have the same meaning?

A The pirates have a plot to take the coastal town.

B The family sold their plot of land on the Hunter River.

C The accuracy with which Jenny can plot points on a graph is amazing.

D I enjoyed the book even though the plot was a bit far fetched.

6 We put the **date** on the document after signing it.

In which sentence does **date** have the same meaning?

A We can date this vase back to the seventeenth century.

B These clothes are so out of date I'd be embarrassed wearing them.

C Our teachers date all work that they mark.

D Each morning I check the date on my wrist watch.

7 We should **match** all the players' names with their team colours.

In which sentence does **match** have the same meaning?

A After the final match all players swapped jerseys.

B Simone's dress was a perfect match with her shoes.

C In Grade 1 students learn to match numbers with counters.

D The Ford was no match for the Toyota on bush tracks.

MINI TEST 2: Words with multiple meanings

For each question, read the sentence and choose the best answer for each question.

1 Each winter the fog will **blanket** the coastal plains.

In which sentence docs **blanket** have the same meaning?

A Gavin added an extra blanket to his bed in winter.

B Snow can blanket the highlands and make roads impassable.

C The principal gave blanket approval to all break-up parties.

D Pull the blanket up before turning out the lights.

2 Until the **code** was broken the soldiers remained in camp.

In which sentence does **code** have the same meaning?

A The postcode for each town in Victoria begins with '3'.

B Connie wrote all her letters in secret code.

C Clubs have a dress code for all members and guests.

D The code book gave a list of symbols used by the enemy.

3 The neighbours share a **common** front driveway.

In which sentence does **common** have the same meaning?

A The cattle were allowed to graze on the town common in Spring.

B In some National Parks palm trees are quite common.

C Most townsfolk thought Colin was common, even ill-mannered.

D There is a common staffroom for both male and female teachers.

4 The **cold** winds swept in from the south all year.

In which sentence does **cold** have the same meaning?

A Luke felt very cold in the mountains of Tasmania.

B The little hut let the cold in from the outside.

C Grandma gave me a cold, hard stare when I asked for money.

D Kathy dropped the cold freezer tray without thinking.

5 When he was four Bobby would **line** up the skittles and knock them down.

In which sentence does **line** have the same meaning?

A The surveyor will line up the pegs for the new playing fields.

B The police were struggling to get a line on the thief.

C In maths class the teacher insisted that every line be neat and straight.

D The troops will line the driveway to the gates or the royal palace.

6 They will plan a **party** when the exams are over.

In which sentence does **party** have the same meaning?

A Mrs Evans became president of the local political party.

B Josie would not be party to such a wild scheme.

C No-one brought presents to the birthday party.

D The party of explorers was lost for ten months in the desert.

7 'Wear a jacket to **ward** off the wind and cold,' said Mum.

In which sentence does **ward** have the same meaning?

A On getting a severe chill the patient was transferred to another ward.

B In the story David became the ward of a kind and loving couple.

C By quick side-stepping the footballer was able to ward off the attack.

D We went into the prison ward and there he was, expecting us!

MINI TEST 1: Interpreting proverbs

For each question, read the proverb and choose the option which best explains it.

These are not too difficult if you understand they are traditional sayings using a form of figurative language. For example:

Proverb: If you pay peanuts, you get monkeys.

This has nothing to do with monkeys or peanuts. It simply means if you pay low wages, you get poor-quality workers.

1   **Proverb:** A leopard does not change its spots.

    A People only change their appearance to get acceptance by others.

    B No matter how people may seem to change, do not trust them.

    C Leopards are not like other cats and will always have spots.

    D People can change but nature remains the same.

2   **Proverb:** One picture is worth a thousand words.

    A More information can be obtained from one picture than from a description.

    B It takes longer to draw a picture than it does to write a story.

    C People who paint pictures are better paid than writers.

    D Pictures cost a lot more than books.

3   **Proverb:** One rotten apple can spoil the whole barrel.

    A If you do not remove any rotten fruit, all the fruit will rot.

    B Keep apples in barrels and the whole lot might become rotten.

    C One bad person in a group may encourage others to follow their example.

    D It is difficult to find criminals because they hide in the lowest places.

4   **Proverb:** Many go out for wool and come home shorn.

    A People who prefer woollen garments will probably accept something else.

    B Some people seek riches and end up losing what they already have.

    C Those who always want the best clothes often come home in rags.

    D If you cannot buy what you want, you might have to make it.

5   **Proverb:** If you play with fire, you will get burnt.

    A Fire is only meant to be used for productive tasks.

    B Anyone who takes unnecessary risks will be hurt.

    C People who play with fire are likely to regret it.

    D Anyone who treats fire as a plaything will be injured.

6   **Proverb:** He who rides a tiger is afraid to dismount.

    A Tiger riding is extremely difficult and dangerous.

    B People who ride animals make them angry and they cannot get off.

    C People who take on outlandish schemes will end up getting hurt.

    D Once a dangerous venture has begun there may be no way of backing out.

7   **Proverb:** If you want peace, you must prepare for war.

    A After every period of peace comes a war.

    B Peaceful countries should not trust any other country.

    C The best time to prepare for war is during times of peace.

    D To live in peace a country must be strong enough to defend itself.

15 min

MINI TEST 2: Interpreting proverbs

For each question, read the proverb and choose the option that best explains it.

1 **Proverb:** New brooms sweep clean.
A New brooms are better than old ones for cleaning.
B Anything new is always better than something old.
C A new person in a job will work hard to get good results.
D If people start off being tidy, they will continue to be tidy.

2 **Proverb:** Eagles don't catch flies.
A Flies are terrible food even for eagles.
B Aggressive people do not eat rubbish food.
C Eagles may be big but they cannot catch small flies.
D Important people do not concern themselves with the trivial.

3 **Proverb:** Throw dirt and some will stick.
A Persistently lie about a person and eventually some lies will be accepted as truth.
B If you throw a lot of dirt around, some of it will make your clothes filthy.
C You cannot expect all the mud to stick to a wall; some will drop off.
D People who throw dirt can expect to get dirty hands.

4 **Proverb:** Don't cross the bridge until you come to it.
A Do not be concerned with difficulties until they arise.
B On any journey do not worry about broken bridges.
C It is impossible to cross a bridge until you reach it.
D If you look for trouble, you will be sure to find it.

5 **Proverb:** Every cloud has a silver lining.
A At sunset even the darkest clouds have bright patches.
B The gloomiest outlook contains some hope.
C If you work hard, you will be rewarded.
D Fine weather always follows storms.

6 **Proverb:** Let sleeping dogs lie.
A People who meddle may cause themselves trouble.
B If a dog is asleep, do not wake it up because it is tired.
C Take care: people can be vicious when woken up.
D Do not trouble yourself with other people's worries.

7 **Proverb:** Give a dog a bad name and hang him.
A A person is innocent until proven guilty.
B If you do not like a dog's name, all you can do is get rid of it.
C Dog owners should not torment their animals—it could kill the animal.
D Ruin a person's reputation and they will eventually behave as predicted.

Mini Test 1

For each question, choose the option that is **least** appropriate when giving a description of the words.

1 a waiter
A courteous
B groomed
C financier
D service

2 a wharf
A ferry
B neutral
C lapping
D passengers

3 a heatwave
A breeze
B swimming
C relentless
D greed

4 sleeping
A dazed
B relaxed
C nodding
D drowse

5 spectator
A match
B anxiety
C victory
D compute

6 the mail
A stamps
B indicator
C delivery
D franking

7 homework
A light
B clock
C cherish
D puzzling

8 the ballet
A impartial
B seating
C effortless
D graceful

9 temptation
A appeal
B obedient
C urge
D conscience

10 school assembly
A seasons
B information
C attentive
D regularly

Mini Test 2

For each question, choose the odd word out in each list.

1
A witness
B observer
C arrested
D onlooker

2
A locality
B home
C neighbourhood
D passengers

3
A imposing
B grand
C striking
D intrusion

4
A secrete
B spy
C conceal
D hide

5
A wild
B untamed
C dingo
D savage

6
A leader
B companion
C friend
D partner

7
A idea
B hint
C imply
D suggest

8
A amusing
B entertaining
C concert
D delighting

9
A wither
B melt
C wilt
D droop

10
A argue
B debate
C quarrel
D wrestle

11
A monitor
B obstacle
C barrier
D construction

12
A tutor
B rouse
C enliven
D inspire

MINI TEST 1: Punctuation

The main punctuation marks used in Year 6 are full stops (.), commas (,), question marks (?), exclamation marks (!), dashes (—), semicolons (;) and speech marks (" " or ' ').

For each question, choose the option which gives the correct punctuation for each of the numbered points in the passage.

'You don't mean that, do you (1)' I argued. I could not believe it.

'Oh, but I do (2) she said, rising from her seat behind the large desk.

'But you promised money (3) maps and some food for the trip. How will we survive? We will freeze to death on the trucks,' I cried with dismay.

She studied my face (4) 'Do you want to stay here?'

'No (5)' I snapped. I could see the snow falling in the yard beyond the window.

1
A comma
B full stop
C question mark
D exclamation mark

2
A full stop
B question mark
C comma and speech marks
D full stop and speech marks

3
A comma
B full stop
C question mark
D exclamation mark

4
A dash
B comma
C full stop
D semicolon

5
A full stop
B question mark
C speech marks
D exclamation mark

55

☞ Answers and explanations on page 77

Mini Test 2

Suddenly Luke was awake. He fumbled for his glasses and perched them on the end of his nose. 'Oh,' he blinked (1) it's only you.'

'Who did you think it was (2) Louise demanded (3) looking anxiously around the room.

'Who knows?', he answered with a wicked smile. 'Maybe a half-crazy monster!'

'That isn't funny (4)', snarled Louise, 'because I've just been chased by a very real-looking mummy.'

'Not possible. Probably was Aunt Fran getting a glass of water.'

Louise glared at him. 'I suppose you think Aunt Fran walks barefoot around the house covered in bandages (5) in the dark!'

1
A comma and speech marks
B full stop and speech marks
C question mark and speech marks
D exclamation mark and speech marks

2
A full stop
B question mark
C full stop and speech marks
D question mark and speech marks

3
A comma
B full stop
C question mark
D exclamation mark

4
A dash
B comma
C semicolon
D exclamation mark

5
A dash
B full stop
C semicolon
D exclamation mark

Mini Test 3

I stumbled through the back door. Mum was getting flustered in the laundry.

'Is that you Michelle (1)' she called. 'You're home nice and early. I was sure tennis finished much later. How did you go?'

For a moment I thought about the trip home then I bowled into the laundry and gave Mum a big hug. I nearly tripped over the jeans (2) tee shirts and jackets on the floor.

Mum looked surprised. 'What's that for?' she asked (3) Not that I'm objecting (4) of course."

'Nothing special.' I grinned sheepishly, 'just (5) thanks.'

1
A comma
B full stop
C question mark
D exclamation mark

2
A dash
B comma
C full stop
D semicolon

3
A comma and speech marks
B full stop and speech marks
C semicolon and speech marks
D question mark and speech marks

4
A dash
B comma
C semicolon
D exclamation mark

5
A dash
B full stop
C semicolon
D exclamation mark

For each question, choose the word that is incorrect.

1 Julie and her **friends where** going roller **skating** at the **new** roller dome.
      A   B   C   D

2 At **their** party the team managed to **break** a saucer, **a** electric kettle and a door **handle**.
      A   B   C   D

3 If it **isn't** thunder and lightning, **it's desert** dust storms turning the sun into a **goldern** ball.
      A   B   C   D

4 **Each one** of the **backpacks** on the bus **are** labelled for security reasons.
      A   B   C   D

5 Jeannie **should of** played in both hockey matches but she **knew** the bus was **leaving**.
             A   B   C   D

6 When the wind starts to **rise** the dog sits in **it's** kennel and growls **softly** at the people passing **by**.
                            A   B   C   D

7 The car went **slow** down towards **their darkened** house at the dangerous **intersection**.
                  A   B   C   D

8 According to the report many men **don't** expect to live longer **then their wives**.
                                    A   B   C   D

9 Mother cried, '**Cant** anyone get it **right** the first time? I **shouldn't** have to **check** everything.'
                  A   B   C   D

10 Our **neighbours**, the Murphy family, sold **apricot's** on a **temporary** stall outside **their** main gate.
         A   B   C   D

For each question, choose the word that is incorrect.

1 Snow White, along with all the **dwarfs**, **were** able to avoid the **wicked witch**.
    Ⓐ   Ⓑ   Ⓒ Ⓓ

2 While driving **passed** the **better restaurant** Charles suddenly slowed and pointed to **its** open door.
    Ⓐ   Ⓑ   Ⓒ   Ⓓ

3 If you use **your** front **break** too much, **you'll** end up having **an** accident on that bicycle.
    Ⓐ   Ⓑ   Ⓒ   Ⓓ

4 The **men** complained that the task of **boring**, sanding and sawing the hard wood beams **are too** difficult.
    Ⓐ   Ⓑ   Ⓒ Ⓓ

5 Marcel should **have** been **grateful** to be considered **for** the team but he was different **to** the other boys.
    Ⓐ   Ⓑ   Ⓒ   Ⓓ

6 Jennifer **definitely offered** to give me a **lend** of the bicycle she **bought** last week.
    Ⓐ   Ⓑ   Ⓒ   Ⓓ

7 Elle ignored the **others'** gathered in the hall and **concentrated her** thoughts on the **mathematics** test.
    Ⓐ   Ⓑ   Ⓒ   Ⓓ

8 Tanya, **along** with her sister, **was** most annoyed when she **seen** the television review of **their** match.
    Ⓐ   Ⓑ   Ⓒ   Ⓓ

9 Twisting my head very **quick** I was **most** surprised to see, **right** before my eyes, an unusual **sight**.
    Ⓐ   Ⓑ   Ⓒ   Ⓓ

10 I **know** I haven't got a ticket **but** I'm not saying **nothing** to you **until** my older sister gets on the bus.
    Ⓐ   Ⓑ   Ⓒ   Ⓓ

10 MIN

For each question, choose the word that is incorrect.

1   Ms Myles **bought** neither groceries **and** cleaning materials **with** her credit card on **Wednesday**.
     Ⓐ   Ⓑ   Ⓒ   Ⓓ

2   Discussions **on** modern music **allways** start heated **arguments** at **our** place.
     Ⓐ   Ⓑ   Ⓒ Ⓓ

3   Children, ten years and under, **aren't aloud** to enter the **area** around the **monkeys'** enclosure.
          Ⓐ Ⓑ   Ⓒ   Ⓓ

4   After a very, **very** long **bout** of influenza Gavin is now feeling **really good**.
     Ⓐ   Ⓑ   Ⓒ Ⓓ

5   All the students, including Rodney, **was hoping** for a class visit to **meet** the **patients**.
          Ⓐ Ⓑ   Ⓒ Ⓓ

6   'When you take **your** swimmers **off** please drop them **into** the washing machine,' **pleadded** Mum.
       Ⓐ   Ⓑ   Ⓒ   Ⓓ

7   **Losing** his wallet **meant** Brett had to get a new bus pass and report the **loss** of his **license**.
 Ⓐ   Ⓑ   Ⓒ Ⓓ

8   My **advise** to you and all your friends **is** to get **a** regular weekend position at **some** fast-food place!
  Ⓐ   Ⓑ Ⓒ   Ⓓ

9   'Why **do** you have difficulties with the exercises **you're** been given?' **asked** the **principal**.
   Ⓐ   Ⓑ   Ⓒ Ⓓ

10 The **childrens'** books **that** won **awards** last year are available **only** in educational book shops.
  Ⓐ   Ⓑ Ⓒ   Ⓓ

MINI TEST 4: Grammar

For each question, choose the word that is incorrect.

1   **Our** plan **was** thrown into confusion when Ross reversed the tractor **backwards across** the street.
Ⓐ   Ⓑ   Ⓒ   Ⓓ

2   It has been **too** wet to mow **either** lawn **for** nine **consecutive** days in a row.
Ⓐ   Ⓑ   Ⓒ   Ⓓ

3   Wendy **angrily teared** up the returned exam paper when she **saw** her poor **results**.
Ⓐ   Ⓑ   Ⓒ   Ⓓ

4   **A** hotel and a **wooden** shed **has** been destroyed in the **service**-station explosion.
Ⓐ   Ⓑ   Ⓒ   Ⓓ

5   That is the most **perfect** present I have **ever** received **for** a birthday since I **was** five.
Ⓐ   Ⓑ   Ⓒ   Ⓓ

6   After the races, jumps and ball games Jenny was **too tied** to climb into **their** car **for** the trip home.
Ⓐ Ⓑ   Ⓒ   Ⓓ

7   The club **sent** a letter **to** you and **I** reminding us to complete **our** applications for membership.
Ⓐ   Ⓑ   Ⓒ   Ⓓ

8   When summer **comes** the whole **scene** was blurred **by** a smoky haze **from** the bushfires in the gully.
Ⓐ   Ⓑ   Ⓒ   Ⓓ

9   I **bought** my sandwich at the canteen and **as** I turned I was **bumped** and dropped **a** sandwich.
Ⓐ   Ⓑ   Ⓒ   Ⓓ

10   **And** so I decided, there and **then**, to tell my brother **just** how to **behave** in my room!
Ⓐ   Ⓑ   Ⓒ   Ⓓ

MINI TEST 5: Grammar

For each question, choose the word that is incorrect.

1 Our street is very **quite**. The only noise we ever **hear** is the **warbling** of **magpies**.
 A · B · C · D

2 The Major **quickly** became **used** to the new town and would wander **daily threw** the parks.
 A · B · C D

3 **Sheeps**, goats, pigs and **emus** were all **raised** on the **higher** areas of land.
 A · B · C · D

4 While **Im** not really sure you can **handle** an axe **I'll** let you try the **tomahawk**.
 A · B · C · D

5 Many **car's** headlights **shone** on the joggers as they **ran** by the **mayor's** statue.
 A · B · C · D

6 Except **for** an old possum in **an** eucalypt tree **there** is nothing that could **have** caused the damage.
 A · B · C · D

7 Trudy arranged **for** Holly, **and** Bindi and Gary **to** have ballet lessons at **separate** times.
 A · B · C · D

8 The judges **were** waiting **for** the **schools'** relay team to join the **others** by the blocks.
 A · B · C · D

9 After the chicken **broke** from **it's** shell the mother hen started **clucking excitedly**.
 A · B · C · D

10 **Without** warning, just **before** the lunch **break**, Alan called out, '**Can** I get the lunch order now?'
 A · B · C · D

For each question, choose the correct word(s) to complete each sentence.

If Eve can ___1___ Ann in this chess match then she will be the ___2___ of the two.

1 A win   B beat   C conquer   D overpower

2 A best   B better   C goodest   D greatest

The tracker dogs were on the ___3___ of criminals ___4___ than Ned Kelly's gang.

3 A sents   B cents   C scents   D sense

4 A worse   B worser   C worest   D most worse

We can ___5___ the police sirens ___6___ from the other side of the harbour.

5 A here   B hear   C hare   D hair

6 A wail   B waile   C whale   D whail

Tina usually watches her favourite ___7___ while ___8___ her daily reports.

7 A cereal   B cerial   C sereal   D serial

8 A writting   B wrighting   C writing   D righting

We watched the baby rock back and ___9___ all ___10___ the night.

9 A fourth   B foreth   C forth   D foureth

10 A through   B threw   C thorough   D few

During King John's ___11___ there were just two years of ___12___ in the valley.

11 A rain   B rein   C reign   D riegn

12 A piece   B peece   C peice   D peace

For Australia to win the event was _____ but to get no-one in a touring team was unusual.

13 A unusually unique   B quite unique   C very unique   D unique

No-one worked at home but Elaine has to travel _____ to work.

14 A furthurest   B more further   C more furtherest   D furthest

We missed the party _____ my brother was involved in an accident.

15 A so   B although   C because   D therefore

Instructions

This is a writing test. You have 30 minutes.

Remember: The amount you write is not as important as the quality of what you write.

If you finish before the time is up, use the remaining time to go over your work and make changes you think might improve it.

It is unwise to work out (memorise) a response before the actual test.

Write a narrative response (story) for the following topic: The party.

Your writing can be:

- based on a real event from personal experience
- imaginary
- amusing or serious
- a first-person narrative (about you)
- a third-person narrative (about other characters).

Remember the **5W questions** as you write: What? When? Who? Where? Why?

Your writing will be judged on:

- what you have to say
- how well organised your response is
- how clearly and effectively you express yourself.

Tips for writing narratives

- When you are asked to write a story in your test, you can write any kind of story you like. It can be **true or imaginary, funny or serious**. There is no single right way to respond. However, you must write on the topic or question you are given. So read the question carefully.

- Whatever kind of story you choose, you should aim to write in an **entertaining and interesting way**. However, the markers know you don't have much time so they won't expect a perfect, polished story. They know it takes more than 30 minutes to write a really good story.

- Even if you are very good at writing stories, remember you will have a lot less time than you usually have. So **practice with a time limit** is very useful.

- There are many different kinds of **stimulus material** used in these tests. For example, you might be given a picture, a story title, or the first or last sentence of a story. Usually the stimulus will allow you to answer in many different ways.

- A common story question is to ask you to **imagine a situation** and to write about it. For example, you might be asked to imagine you are a different kind of person, an animal or an object, and to write about what your life is like. We will look at these *Imagine if...* stories in this session.

- For these *Imagine if...* stories you have to really **use your imagination** but the question is very open so you have plenty of opportunity to show your ideas. It is usually best to choose a topic that you know something about so you can quickly come up with some good ideas.

- Other questions lead you directly to a **narrative story** (a story about people and what they do, or what happens to them). Your own experiences are very useful when writing these narrative stories—especially in test conditions.

- Avoid clichéd endings such as *I woke up and it was all a dream* or *They lived happily ever after.*

- Direct speech is a feature of many narratives. Quoted words require quotation marks (' ').

General tips

- Make use of relevant, but limited, literary techniques such as rhetorical questions (Who could do such a thing?) and exclamations (Don't believe it!).

- Vary your sentence length and sentence beginnings.

- You will be writing under test conditions but make every effort to spell common words correctly. Some allowance is made for the incorrect spelling of unusual or technical words.

- Make sure your punctuation is correct and that you make good use of vocabulary.

- Keep your handwriting legible.

- Give yourself a minute or two at the end to read through your work. This is the time to check spelling and punctuation and to put in words that have been accidentally left out.

- Don't forget you only have 30 minutes to complete this task.

30 MIN

Instructions

This is a writing test. You have 30 minutes.

Remember: The amount you write is not as important as the quality of what you write.

If you finish before the time is up, use the remaining time to go over your work and make changes you think might improve it.

It is unwise to work out (memorise) a response before the actual test.

Write a newspaper report about an interesting and exciting discovery.

It can:

- be something natural—animal, plant or mineral
- be an invention, a new way of doing something or something lost
- be a public reaction
- concern a location of significance
- contain a historical perspective
- include comments from local people and professional observers
- detail how it affected locals/visitors to the area.

Remember the **5W questions** as you write: What? When? Who? Where? Why?

Your writing will be judged on:

- what you have to say
- how well organised your response is
- how clearly and effectively you express yourself.

Tips for writing newspaper reports

Newspaper reports are recounts for a specific purpose.

A recount retells an experience or event that **has already happened**. The purpose of a recount can be to inform, to entertain, to reflect or to evaluate.

A factual or newspaper recount reports the particulars of an incident by reconstructing factual information. A newspaper recount is an objective (impersonal) recount of a true event by someone not personally involved in the situation. Its purpose is to inform and, at times, entertain.

Newspaper reports:

- include facts. Think about answering the **5W questions**: What? When? Who? Where? Why?
- provide a summary at the start explaining what happened (but holding back some facts)
- group relevant information in paragraphs
- use short one- or two-sentence paragraphs to help readers clearly understand the information and to hold their interest
- convey people's opinions or comments in indirect speech. If a person's actual words about the event are used to give impact or to lend credibility to the report, these words should be enclosed in quotation marks
- usually describe events in chronological order (first, next, during, after, later, eventually).

Your writing should also:
- focus only on significant information
- be formal (written as though you're talking to someone who wants to be informed)
- use third-person pronouns (he, she, it, they)
- be written in the past tense because the events have already happened.

You may also include:
- a personal comment: What did you think or feel? What have you decided is relevant about the event?
- personal opinions or interpretations (of informed people) about the event
- a short, attention-catching and informative headline.

General tips

- Make use of relevant, but limited, literary techniques such as rhetorical questions (Who could do such a thing?) and exclamations (Don't believe it!).
- Vary your sentence length and sentence beginnings.
- You will be writing under test conditions but make every effort to spell common words correctly. Some allowance is made for the incorrect spelling of unusual or technical words.
- Make sure your punctuation is correct and that you make good use of vocabulary.
- Keep your handwriting legible.
- Give yourself a minute or two at the end to read through your work. This is the time to check spelling and punctuation and to add words that have been accidentally left out.
- Don't forget you only have 30 minutes to complete this task.

Instructions

This is a writing test. You have 30 minutes.

Remember: The amount you write is not as important as the quality of what you write.

If you finish before the time is up, use the remaining time to go over your work and make changes you think might improve it.

It is unwise to work out (memorise) a response before the actual test.

Write a persuasive text response for this topic: School cooking classes should be discontinued.

You can include the following:

- examples based on personal experience
- a forceful presentation of your opinion
- imagery (figurative language)
- amusing or serious writing
- facts gained from other people and sources
- references to research and common knowledge
- emotive language.

Five persuasive techniques

- Establish trust and develop credibility. Sound as if you believe what you are writing.
- Understand the reader's purpose and align this to your own.
- Pay attention to language.
- Consider tone.
- Use rhetoric, repetition and other literary techniques.
- Remember the **5W questions** as you write: What? When? Who? Where? Why?

Your writing will be judged on:

- what you have to say
- how well organised your response is
- how clearly and effectively you express yourself.

SAMPLE TEST 3

Tips for writing persuasive texts

Persuasive texts (expositions or opinions) are used to 'argue' the case for or against a particular action or point of view; to persuade others to see it your way. Such texts need to be well organised and clear. If not, the reader will not follow the ideas and will not be convinced by your point of view.

The stimulus prompt for a persuasive text may be posed as a question or as a statement. This means your writing can draw upon your personal experience. Decide quickly if you are for or against the topic. Remember to sound confident.

- Give your opinion on the topic. Do you agree or disagree? Is X a good idea or a bad idea?
- Remember: The stance you take in a persuasive text is not wrong, as long as you have included evidence to support your opinion. How the opinion is supported is as important as the opinion itself.
- Good persuasive texts often use impersonal writing. However, it is not uncommon for personal opinions to be part of the text.
- Right from the beginning it is important to present the position you have taken: what you stand for. This might be in the title, the first line or the first paragraph of your response.
- Persuasive texts have a tight structure. Your reasons must be logical and easily understood. Persuasive texts make arguments (points) and give evidence to support them.
- Paragraphing is important. Use paragraphs with topic sentences to organise your information. Use a new paragraph for each new idea. Without paragraphs your arguments become difficult to follow.
- Arguments are ordered according to your choice. They can be 'numbered', (firstly, secondly, finally). The final paragraph restates your position forcefully and wraps up your case. It can include a recommendation.
- Only use arguments (or points) that add to your case. 'Waffle' and unnecessary detail won't improve a persuasive text. Once you have made a point there is no need to repeat it.
- Use interesting, precise words and strong persuasive words such as *must* and *believe*.
- As your writing may include personal opinion, avoid too many sentences starting with *I*.
- Direct speech is not a feature of persuasive texts. Indirect speech (reported speech) does not have quotation marks.

General tips
- Persuasive texts are usually written in the present tense.
- Make use of relevant, but limited, literary techniques such as rhetorical questions (Who could do such a thing?), exclamations (Don't believe it!) and italics (*his* opinion, really?).
- Vary your sentence length and sentence beginnings.
- You will be writing under test conditions but make every effort to spell common words correctly. Some allowance is made for the incorrect spelling of unusual or technical words.
- Make sure your punctuation is correct and that you make good use of vocabulary.
- Keep your handwriting legible.
- Give yourself a minute or two at the end to read through your work. This is the time to check spelling and punctuation and to add words that have been accidentally left out.
- Don't forget you only have 30 minutes to complete this task.

SAMPLE TEST 4

Instructions

This is a writing test. You have 30 minutes.

Choose one of the following and write a personal recount:

- a visit to a new and interesting natural feature, such as a remote waterfall, an isolated headland, an islet, a dry salt lake or a bush swimming hole
- an unexpected meeting of an interesting/unusual person
- your first bushwalk
- competing in a long-distance race (such as running, swimming, sailing or cycling)
- a skateboard incident.

Before you start to write, think about:

- where and when the recount takes place
- the events that take place in your recount and the issues they raise
- how you (or others) felt or reacted about the event—you may comment on the events as you write about them.

Remember to:

- plan your personal recount before you start writing
- write in correctly formed sentences and take care with paragraphing
- pay attention to vocabulary, spelling and punctuation
- write neatly but don't waste time
- quickly check your writing once you have finished.

Tips for writing recounts

A recount is the retelling of an event. It usually tells the events in the order the incidents happened: the chronological order.

A personal recount involves the writer's personal experiences and uses the personal pronouns *I* and *we*. Take care not to overuse the personal pronoun *I*, especially as a sentence beginning.

Personal recounts:

- are written in the first person
- use the past tense (Present tense can be used for reactions and opinion.)
- use proper nouns to refer to specific people, places, times and events
- include conjunctions and connectives to link events and indicate time sequence. Because recounts can record either events that happen over a short period or events that happen over a lifetime, you need conjunctions and connectives to link and order these events. Take care not to overuse the adverb of time *then*, especially as a sentence beginning
- feature a variety of sentence lengths and beginnings to sustain the reader's interest
- include figurative language, such as similes and metaphors, where appropriate. Try to avoid clichés
- end with a conclusion. This tells how the experience ended. You may give your opinion about what happened and some thoughts you may have had about the experience. A rhetorical question can be used to encourage the reader to reflect on your experience.

Your writing should also:

- quickly explain the who, what, when, and where of the experience in your introduction to your recount to orient the reader
- focus mainly on events or observations that add to your recount. Events are often described in the sequence in which they occurred
- organise relevant chronological events into paragraphs. You need to start a new paragraph when there is a change in time or place, or a new idea
- add personal comments, opinions or thoughts about the experience.

General tips

- When you have finished writing, give yourself a few moments to read through your recount. Quickly check spelling and punctuation and insert words that have been accidentally left out.
- You will be writing under test conditions but make every effort to spell common words correctly. Some allowance is made for the incorrect spelling of unusual or technical words.
- Make sure your punctuation is correct and that you make good use of vocabulary.
- Keep your handwriting legible. Don't forget you only have 30 minutes to complete this task.

Checklist for writing narratives

Did the student:

- write at least one sentence to orient the reader and capture their imagination?

- include a 'catchy' beginning?

- include an event that adds interest to the story and makes it worth telling?

- resolve the story in a satisfying way?

- use vivid, interesting images to describe people, places, things and activities, such as verbs, adverbs and adjectives?

- use appropriate grammar, punctuation and spelling?

- include a variety of sentence beginnings and lengths?

- use figurative literary techniques such as similes, metaphors, alliteration, rhetorical questions and repetition?

- include relevant descriptions?

- make the narrative flow?

- create ongoing tension to make the reader want to read on?

- provide a satisfying conclusion?

- have a handwriting style that was legible?

Checklist for writing newspaper reports

Did the student:

- choose an interesting subject/topic?

- generate a 'catchy' headline?

- orient the reader to who, what, where and when?

- write in the past tense?

- use the third person?

- use short, well-spaced paragraphs?

- include interesting details?

- use vivid, interesting images to describe people, places, things and activities, such as verbs, adverbs and adjectives?

- use appropriate grammar, punctuation and spelling?

- add personal comments and/or comments by interested parties about what happened?

- distinguish between direct speech and reported speech?

- use time words and expressions to allow the reader to follow the sequence of events?

- use figurative journalistic techniques such as similes, metaphors, alliteration, rhetorical questions and repetition?

- write a concluding comment?

- have a handwriting style that was legible?

CHECKLISTS

Checklist for writing persuasive texts

Did the student:

- make the issue clear from the beginning?
- provide a clear statement of their opinion (using the first person)?
- make their points flow clearly and logically?
- develop arguments using facts and examples?
- arouse any feelings or reactions in the reader?
- use clear paragraphs for each point?
- use appropriate grammar, punctuation and spelling?
- use personal pronouns correctly?
- include a variety of sentence beginnings?
- use interesting verbs, adverbs and adjectives?
- use figurative literary techniques such as similes, metaphors, alliteration, rhetorical questions and repetition?
- make you want to read on?
- suggest and challenge any alternative opinions?
- restate the original assertion clearly as part of the conclusion?
- have a handwriting style that was legible?

Checklist for writing recounts

Did the student:

- quickly let the reader know where, when and who was involved?
- include an intriguing/interesting location?
- include incidents that add interest to the recount and make it worth retelling?
- provide a thought-provoking conclusion?
- use vivid, interesting images to describe people, places, things and activities, such as verbs, adverbs and adjectives?
- use appropriate grammar, punctuation and spelling?
- include a variety of sentence beginnings and lengths?
- use some figurative literary techniques such as similes, metaphors, alliteration, rhetorical questions and repetition?
- incorporate some factual text to provide a sense of authenticity?
- include relevant descriptions?
- include chronological features (e.g. adverbs of time) that keep the narrative flowing?
- create an ongoing issue to encourage the reader to read on?
- make the characters realistic?
- have a handwriting style that was legible?

Answers and selected explanations

Mini Test 1
Page 1

1 B 2 C 3 B 4 C 5 D 6 A

When in doubt read the line slowly, in your mind, and think about the logic of the various options.

2 Take care with prepositions (near, by, off, etc.) and conjunctions (joining words).

4 'And' and 'but' are conjunctions; 'that' is used to introduce a phrase. 'What' is often incorrectly used in such situations.

6 You have to check back a few lines to get the most appropriate word. Sometimes you have to read forward to get the right word.

Mini Test 2
Page 2

1 D 2 C 3 D 4 C 5 A 6 A 7 C

Questions 3 and 4 require an intelligent interpretation of the passage. A number of options could seem satisfactory but students need to select the best option.

7 'Traps' and 'catches' are incorrect because they are similar to 'captures' in the text; 'kills' is not right as the prey must first be captured.

Mini Test 3
Page 3

1 A 2 B 3 C 4 C 5 D 6 B 7 A 8 C

1 'What' is not acceptable English in this situation—'who' is best as it refers to people.

4 All answers may seem right but you must remember that Deidre is on a slope.

5 This becomes obvious if you read forward to the second-last line where a second coffin is mentioned.

Mini Test 4
Page 4

1 B 2 C 3 C 4 C 5 B 6 A 7 A 8 D

3 This requires some care. 'Loomed' (C) best fits the style of the passage, although 'got' could be right. 'Become' is grammatically incorrect. For B to be acceptable it would have to be 'became'.

6 'Peered' is best because it implies a very active concern or interest.

7 The preceding sentence is concerned with 'life'.

Mini Test 5
Page 5

1 C 2 A 3 C 4 B 5 B 6 A 7 C

Read the whole poem through at least once before you start. Get a feel for it and look for any clues that might help you understand it, including title and pictures.

1 here's = here is

2 In stanza two you have to read the second line to realise the word must rhyme with 'go' (toe).

3 The clowns are not on a bus. They are on foot. 'March' in this line is used in the sense of progressing but 'procession' is not really correct English.

4 Another rhyming word means there are two choices. They are being watched by a giggle-goggling 'crowd'.

5 'Paint' is the most appropriate word. Clowns have painted faces which hide their feelings.

7 There are four rhyming words to choose from. 'Cantering' is a type of galloping along, so 'come' is the best word.

Mini Test 6
Page 6

1 D 2 C 3 B 4 C 5 B 6 D 7 A 8 D

4   A and B could be right but they are not strong enough for the passage.

5   This takes some thought. If there is no 'growing' then there can be no 'flowering', 'seeding' or 'germinating.'

7   'Clay' and 'bones' are unlikely. We usually think of dust settling (A). The amounts of 'iridium' would be too small to notice.

Mini Test 7
Page 7

1 B 2 A 3 D 4 A 5 A 6 A 7 A 8 B

1   This requires you to read on to get the answer that fits the overall meaning of the text. The second paragraph is about dreaming.

8   'Gently' is correct—the other options imply a possibility of startling the sleepwalker, which is something dealt with in the sentence following.

Mini Test 8
Page 8

1 A 2 C 3 D 4 D 5 A 6 A 7 B 8 D

1   'Running' in this context carries the meaning of unwinding as well as following a particular course.

4   'Exactly' is the best word because it is repeated for effect in the next part of the sentence.

7   'I' could work but the next phrase starts with 'we' and as there are two of them it is the best word.

Mini Test 9
Page 9

1 B 2 D 3 A 4 D 5 B 6 B 7 A

Questions 4 and 5 require the right shade of meaning. All could be acceptable but they must fit the mood and style of the passage. For question 4 we can assume that for most of his trip he crossed uninhabited lands. The other words indicate the land was occupied—at least at one time.

6   This refers to the type of climate generally— not specifically that of Iceland. Though the people may also be poor and courageous, 'hardy' is the best choice.

7   This becomes obvious when you read on.

Mini Test 10
Page 10

1 A 2 B 3 C 4 A 5 C 6 D 7 B 8 B

1   If you read on you will find 'debt' is the best answer, although 'bill' and 'account' may be possible.

7   All options are possible. 'Cheat' is the best option because it shows the moneylender's evil intent more than 'trickster'.

8   'Lost' is the best option but it is using 'lost' in a specific way.

Mini Test 11
Page 6

1 B 2 A 3 C 4 A 5 D 6 B 7 C 8 B

5   The previous sentence emphasises the sound of the event.

6   'Instants' is not correct. An instant refers to a very precise point of time.

Mini Test 12
Page 12

1 C 2 C 3 D 4 B 5 A 6 A 7 B 8 D 9 A

3   'Looked' is the best option as it is repeated, for effect, later in the sentence.

4   At this stage of the strange events there is nothing 'frantic' happening but it is starting to 'puzzle'.

5   Dave took a 'weapon' but his weapon was a stick of firewood. A 'bundle' or 'block' would be impractical.

7   These are all adverbs. Dave could not meow noiselessly—'presently' implies he had to wait a while, which suits the situation that is developing.

Mini Test 13
Page 13

1 C 2 C 3 A 4 D 5 A 6 A 7 C 8 B 9 C

1 'Allowed' is correct; it is explained in the next sentence. To become an astronaut, a person had to be a pilot in the army or navy. Women were not allowed to be pilots.

4 The exclamation mark implies that a stronger word than 'hoped' and 'sighed' is required— 'smirked' is not consistent with her genuine feeling of frustration.

7 'Cargo' includes almost everything on board. The word must be more specific. People are not cargo.

Mini Test 14
Page 14

1 B 2 A 3 C 4 C 5 B 6 C 7 D 8 A 9 A

1 'had … seen' not 'had … saw'

4 'Swim' is the wrong tense.

8 Tunnels and doorways can be considered 'made by people'. In this environment a more natural feature is required—a 'crack'. A 'depression' is a dip or hollow.

9 'Well over' makes the entrance size much less of a problem and is not in keeping with the implied difficulties.

Mini Test 15
Page 15

1 C 2 C 3 A 4 A 5 A 6 C 7 D 8 C

In this passage do not let the foreign words put you off.

1 This is an example of a question where, if you read on, the answer becomes obvious.

3 There are nine numbers to be added but 'nine' is grammatically incorrect.

6 Take care with 'past' (has happened) and 'passed' (went).

7 As they are magic squares, they would be regarded as 'magical'.

Mini Test 16
Page 16

1 B 2 D 3 A 4 C 5 C 6 B 7 A 8 D

2 'Assignment' is the only option (it starts with a vowel) as it is preceded by 'an'.

3 The correct answer is 'texts', which is another name for books.

8 'Embossed' implies the initials will be slightly raised—gold added to the surface of the diary would raise them slightly.

Mini Test 17
Page 17

1 B 2 D 3 A 4 C 5 D 6 D 7 A 8 A 9 B

1 Tanks may seem right but this is only spoken hypothetically ('if tanks …'). Read on and you will see the passage is about an attack on trucks.

3 'Bright' is inappropriate. The dull lights had a purpose so they were not entirely 'useless'. 'Sinister' would be appropriate if the attackers had been threatened.

5 'Cutting' is the best option as they are waiting on top of a cutting—see the second paragraph.

9 'Strips' is best. When something is shredded it is usually torn into ragged strips rather than broken up into 'lumps'.

Spelling tests (pages 19–37)

INCORRECT SPELLING

Mini Test 1
Page 19

1 D 2 B 3 C 4 C 5 A 6 C 7 D 8 B 9 C 10 D

Mini Test 2
Page 19

1 D 2 D 3 C 4 A 5 D 6 B 7 A 8 B 9 B 10 D

Mini Test 3
Page 20

1 B 2 A 3 C 4 C 5 D 6 C 7 D 8 D 9 B 10 B

Mini Test 4 — Page 20
1 A 2 B 3 A 4 D 5 A 6 D 7 C 8 D 9 C 10 D

Mini Test 5 — Page 21
1 B 2 D 3 C 4 A 5 C 6 D 7 D 8 A 9 C 10 D

Mini Test 6 — Page 21
1 D 2 A 3 D 4 D 5 A 6 C 7 C 8 B 9 D 10 A

Mini Test 7 — Page 22
1 A 2 C 3 C 4 A 5 B 6 D 7 C 8 B 9 A 10 C

Mini Test 8 — Page 22
1 A 2 B 3 C 4 B 5 D 6 D 7 C 8 A 9 D 10 D

Mini Test 9 — Page 23
1 D 2 C 3 D 4 D 5 D 6 C 7 A 8 C 9 A 10 D

Mini Test 10 — Page 23
1 A 2 D 3 D 4 A 5 C 6 B 7 B 8 A 9 A 10 B

Mini Test 11 — Page 24
1 D 2 C 3 B 4 A 5 D 6 D 7 D 8 A 9 B 10 C

Mini Test 12 — Page 24
1 B 2 A 3 D 4 D 5 D 6 B 7 A 8 C 9 A 10 C

FINDING ERRORS

Mini Test 1 — Page 25
1 C 2 A 3 C 4 C 5 B

Mini Test 2 — Page 26
1 B 2 D 3 A 4 D 5 C

Mini Test 3 — Page 27
1 B 2 D 3 A 4 B 5 D

Mini Test 4 — Page 28
1 C 2 B 3 A 4 D 5 C

Mini Test 5 — Page 29
1 A 2 A 3 D 4 B 5 A

Mini Test 6 — Page 30
1 A 2 D 3 A 4 C 5 C

Mini Test 7 — Page 31
1 B 2 D 3 A 4 C 5 A

Mini Test 8 — Page 32
1 D 2 B 3 D 4 C 5 A

SPELLING/EDITING

Mini Test 1 — Page 33
Answers
1. A Principal C worst D idiot F prison
2. A always B brooding C he's D Personally E to
3. A does B atlases D cupboard E there
4. B before C agony E stifled F protection

Mini Test 2 — Page 34
Answers
1. A tufts C goal D staring F whole
2. B gallery C past D patterns E panes
3. A Library B whose D services F currently
4. A handsome B military C guard D ignore E excellent

ALPHABETICAL ORDER

Mini Test 1 — Page 35
1 B 2 A 3 B 4 C 5 A 6 D 7 B 8 B 9 B

Mini Test 2 — Page 36
1 B 2 C 3 A 4 B 5 D 6 A 7 C 8 D 9 A

Mini Test 3 — Page 37
1 A 2 B 3 D 4 C 5 A 6 D 7 B 8 A 9 D

Vocabulary tests (pages 39–54)

SYNONYMS

Mini Test 1 — Page 39

1 D 2 C 3 D 4 A 5 A 6 B 7 A 8 B 9 C

Mini Test 2 — Page 40

1 A 2 A 3 B 4 B 5 A 6 C 7 A 8 C 9 A

Mini Test 3 — Page 41

1 C 2 D 3 A 4 C 5 D 6 C 7 B 8 D 9 C

Mini Test 4 — Page 42

1 C 2 C 3 C 4 B 5 B 6 A 7 C 8 C 9 D

Mini Test 5 — Page 43

1 B 2 D 3 C 4 B 5 B 6 A 7 A 8 D 9 D

Mini Test 6 — Page 44

1 A 2 D 3 B 4 C 5 C 6 C 7 B 8 A 9 C

Mini Test 7 — Page 45

1 D 2 C 3 C 4 B 5 B 6 B 7 C 8 D 9 A

Mini Test 8 — Page 46

1 C 2 B 3 B 4 C 5 D 6 A 7 C 8 B 9 C

Mini Test 9 — Page 47

1 A 2 A 3 A 4 B 5 B 6 C 7 B 8 D 9 B

ANTONYMS

Mini Test 1 — Page 48

1 A 2 C 3 C 4 A 5 B 6 A 7 B 8 D 9 D

Mini Test 2 — Page 49

1 B 2 A 3 A 4 C 5 C 6 A 7 B 8 D 9 A

WORDS WITH MULTIPLE MEANINGS

Mini Test 1 — Page 50

1 A 2 D 3 C 4 D 5 C 6 D 7 C

Mini Test 2 — Page 51

1 B 2 B 3 D 4 D 5 A 6 C 7 C

INTERPRETING PROVERBS

These are not too difficult if you understand they are traditional sayings using a form of figurative language.

Mini Test 1 — Page 52

1 B 2 A 3 C 4 B 5 B 6 D 7 D

Mini Test 2 — Page 53

1 C 2 D 3 A 4 A 5 B 6 A 7 D

WORD ASSOCIATIONS

Mini Test 1 — Page 54

1 C 2 B 3 D 4 A 5 D 6 B 7 C 8 A 9 B 10 A

Mini Test 2 — Page 54

1 C 2 D 3 D 4 B 5 C 6 A 7 A 8 C 9 B
10 D 11 A 12 A

Punctuation tests (pages 55–56)

Mini Test 1 — Page 55

1 C 2 C 3 A 4 C 5 D

5   A comma may work but is not appropriate punctuation for 'snapped'.

Mini Test 2 — Page 56

1 A 2 D 3 A 4 D 5 A

Mini Test 3 — Page 56

1 C 2 B 3 B 4 B 5 A

Note: Speech marks can be written as double (" ") or single (' '). Many primary-school teachers still prefer double speech marks.

Grammar tests (pages 57–62)

Mini Test 1
Page 57

1 B 2 C 3 D 4 D 5 B 6 B 7 A 8 B 9 A 10 B

Explanations

1 **were** not where
2 **an** electric
3 spelling: golden
4 Each one ... **is**
5 should **have**
6 **its** not it's (it is)
7 slowly
8 **than** not then
9 Can't
10 **apricots** not apricot's (no apostrophe)

Mini Test 2
Page 58

1 B 2 A 3 B 4 C 5 D 6 C 7 A 8 C 9 A 10 C

Explanations

1 Snow White ... was
2 spelling: past
3 spelling: brake
4 task ... was (tense)
5 different **from**
6 loan (noun)—lend is a verb
7 others—no apostrophe
8 saw
9 slow**ly** (adverb)
10 not saying **anything**

Mini Test 3
Page 59

1 B 2 B 3 B 4 D 5 A 6 D 7 D 8 A 9 B 10 A

Explanations

1 neither—**nor**
2 spelling: always
3 spelling: allowed
4 really **well**
5 students ... were
6 spelling: pleaded
7 spelling: licence
8 advice (noun)
9 you'**ve** (you have)
10 children's (plural possession)

Mini Test 4
Page 60

1 C 2 D 3 B 4 C 5 A 6 B 7 C 8 A 9 D 10 A

Explanations

1 If the tractor reversed, it was backwards. Therefore backwards is unnecessay (tautology) so delete backwards.
2 Consecutive means in a row (tautology) so delete consecutive.
3 tore
4 have (plural verb)

5 **Most** perfect is impossible (nothing is better than perfect!). A better word would be 'exciting', or just leave out 'most' and use **best**!
6 spelling: tired
7 the club sent a letter to ... me
8 came (tense)
9 **the** sandwich (definite article)
10 **And** is a conjunction and not (correctly) used for sentence beginnings (sometimes, though, it may be used for literary/dramatic effect in stories and poems).

Mini Test 5
Page 61

1 A 2 D 3 A 4 A 5 A 6 B 7 B 8 C 9 B 10 D

Explanations

1 quiet
2 through
3 Sheep is both singular and plural.
4 I'm
5 There are many cars so the apostrophe should be after the 's': cars'.
6 The 'e' in eucalypt does not have a vowel sound.
7 Delete **and** entirely as the comma is used on its own in this series.
8 School is singular so the apostrophe goes before the 's'.
9 It's is short for it is; its is the correct word.
10 'May' is the correct word meaning to ask for permission. 'Can' asks if someone is able to.

Mini Test 6
Page 62

1 B 2 B 3 C 4 A 5 B 6 A 7 D 8 C 9 C
10 A 11 C 12 D 13 D 14 D 15 C

Selected Explanations

2 'Better' should always be used when comparing two objects or people.
4 'Worest' is not a word. If comparing two groups, use 'worse'.
13 If something is 'unique', it is the only one of its kind and cannot be used in comparisons.

Language and ideas

Vocabulary

Good use is made of unusual words, adverbs of time, verbs and adjectives.

Sentence structure

A wide variety of sentence beginnings and lengths is included.

Direct speech keeps the storyline flowing.

Most sentences are statements.

Ideas

A **simile** gives a clear picture of the character's emotional state.

A rhetorical question sustains the tension.

Punctuation

Questions are used to highlight frustrations.

Exclamation marks are used to increase the sense of urgency in making a decision.

This sentence suggests a solution may be possible.

A one-word sentence is used for dramatic effect.

Spelling

There are no spelling errors of common, unusual or technical words.

Writing Test 1: sample answer

The Party

On Tuesday I found a letter from Amanda Redman in our letterbox. It was an unexpected invitation for me!

I was invited to a red, fancy-dress party on Saturday afternoon. Your costume must be 'red'! A prize for the most original red costume. I showed the invitation to Mum and Dad.

'Looks like fun Tim,' said Dad. 'What can you be that's red?'

Suddenly I couldn't think of anything.

Mum said, 'How about the Little Red Engine?'

Dad laughed. 'A red robin?' I didn't like those woeful ideas. They wouldn't win a prize!

'If you were a girl, you could go as Little Red Riding Hood,' chuckled Mum. We had run out of ideas. 'Let's have a rest and try again tomorrow.' Tomorrow was Wednesday.

Wednesday was no better. We came up with red Martian and even a red tomato! Our ideas were getting bizarre and Saturday was getting closer.

Thursday was no better. On Friday we had no ideas at all. I was drained of ideas. **I was as glum as a lost puppy.**

On Saturday morning we were all glum. Dad said, 'I'm going for the newspaper. I can't help. Sorry Tim.'

Then Mum looked at me in a funny way and smiled. She had an idea.

At the party there were three Little Red Riding Hoods, one red fox and a Little Red Hen. All the kids stared at my costume. They looked puzzled. Amanda was a Red Cross nurse. Pointing at my costume she said, 'That's not even a bit red Tim!'

The kids stopped smiling but I smiled. 'I'm a newspaper,' I explained, 'because they might be black and white but they are definitely read!'

It took a brief moment for her to understand.

Guess who got the prize? Me! The prize was a book. That should be read too!

Please note that this sample has not been written under test conditions. During a test you might not have the time to produce such a polished piece of writing. However, this sample gives you a standard to aim for.

Structure

Audience

The topic is one that would be familiar to readers. The writer quickly specifies location and time frame.

An issue to be resolved is introduced.

It is written in the first person (I).

Text structure

Days of the week are used to show time running out to resolve the problem.

The story has an easy-to-follow chronological sequence.

The narrative focuses on specific events.

Paragraphing

New paragraphs are used for changes in speakers, in time and in place.

Cohesion

The writer's intention is established early.

The situation now seems hopeless.

The story has an obvious beginning, middle and end.

The final sentences demonstrate quickly how the problem was solved in a satisfying way for the reader.

The narrative goes from excitement to increasing desperation to a successful conclusion.

The last sentence (coda) neatly rounds off the narrative with a pun.

Structure

Audience
The audience is readers interested in dinosaurs.

The writer quickly establishes the issue, actual location and climatic situation.

Text structure
The article deals with a scientific issue but gives it a personal touch.

Points are raised to give credence to the relevance of the article.

The article is written in the past tense.

Professional opinion is sought.

The report focuses on specific information.

Paragraphing
Paragraphs are short and focus on one point but may include some support detail.

Cohesion
The writer's intention is established early: to inform in an objective manner.

The final paragraphs stress the relevant global importance of the discovery.

Writing Test 2: sample answer

Dinosaurs Down Under

The largest dinosaur skeleton ever found in Australia belongs to a newly discovered species.

Known as *Australotitan cooperensis*, the basketball-court-length dinosaur's remains were first found and excavated in the outback of Queensland in 2006 and 2007.

The animal's English name, Southern Titan of the Cooper, or Cooper, is a tribute to the freshwater Cooper Creek close to where it was found.

Scientists say Cooper is an entirely newly discovered species of long-necked titanosaur dinosaur that lived around 95 million years ago. Cooper grazed on plants,, weighed about 70 tonnes, reached nearly 30 metres in length and stood **as high as a two-story building!**

For more than 15 years, museum experts from the Eromanga Museum, along with other paleontologists, geologists and volunteers, worked to identify the findings and confirm it was a unique species. This involved painstaking work excavating the fragile remains and removing the large rock in which the bones had been entombed.

'The discovery of Cooper was totally unexpected. Since then, numerous dinosaur discoveries have followed and continue to be made,' Eromanga Museum and field paleontologist Robyn Mackenzie said.

The discoveries have opened a whole new world, not just for her family, but for Australia generally.

The journey began fortuitously for Mackenzie in 2004, when her son, Sandy, found a rock reminiscent of a fossil on their property near Cooper Creek. The family had long thought there could be dinosaurs below their home — and the discovery set them on a mission to find out. They've since built a foundation and a museum in the area.

Queensland's outback is comprised of flat plains which can make finding dinosaur remains trickier than in mountainous or other terrains where earth more easily erodes and fossils are exposed.

'Cooper is the first Australian dinosaur to join the elite group of giant dinosaurs,' Mackenzie said. 'They are the largest dinosaurs that ever walked on Earth and, based on the preserved limb-size comparisons, this new titanosaur is estimated to be in the top five largest in the world!'

Most other dinosaurs of Cooper's massive calibre were found in South America.

Adapted from https://www.washingtonpost.com/world/2021/06/08/australia-new-dinosaur-australotitan-cooperensis

Please note that this sample has not been written under test conditions. During a test you might not have the time to produce such a polished piece of writing, of course.

Language and ideas

Vocabulary
Good use of unusual words, adverbs of time, pronouns and adjectives.

Scientific terms provide authenticity.

Sentence structure
The importance of the event is brought home by the opening sentence.

There is a wide variety of sentence beginnings.

Reported information is incorporated into the text.

A **simile** is used to good effect. The actual words spoken are in speech marks.

Most sentences are statements, either simple or compound.

Ideas
Alliteration gives the text a catchy title.

There is a clever balance of personal and professional facts.

Punctuation
Clear use is made of dashes and commas.

Some restrained use is made of exclamations.

The last line rounds off the point made in the first line and gives a context to the discovery.

Spelling
There are no spelling errors of common, unusual or technical words.

Structure

Audience

The topic is one that would be familiar to students and parents.

The writer quickly and forcefully establishes the issue and their stance.

The first person is used.

Text structure

Points are organised sequentially, including numbering.

The text contains a well-organised introduction, support points and a conclusion.

Positive words are used throughout the text (certainly, better, proper).

Paragraphing

New paragraphs are used for each new point.

A topic sentence is used to introduce the paragraph's main idea.

Cohesion

The writer's intention is established early.

The writer refers regularly to words used in the topic.

The present tense is used.

Personal experience is used to bolster the position taken.

The final paragraph refers to the topic and re-establishes how the writer feels.

The text ends with a strong, personal reaffirmation of the writer's opinion.

The concluding sentence rounds off the stance taken in the opening paragraph.

School cooking classes should be discontinued

One can only wonder why schools continue with cooking classes. How can they be justified?

Just to put the issue into perspective: fewer people cook 'proper' meals these days. Why should they? The supermarkets have prepacked, chilled, frozen or ready-to-eat meals across many aisles. Pasta—just pop it in the microwave and hey presto! Cooked chook from the hot chicken counter. No home cooking needed. And how many young adults bother to shop, cook and wash up when there are takeaway outlets nearby. Cooking was for my grandparents.

Secondly it can be argued that cooking in schools is a waste of time. This time could be better used for the 'three Rs': reading, writing and 'rithmetic. These *are* the subjects that will prepare students for the real world. There's little you can do with cooking unless you want to be a chef.

Those who support cooking lessons say the students get opportunities to learn practical skills such as weighing and measuring. These skills, however, can be taught and practised in science and maths lessons. Much more relevant! Then there's the claim that cooking teaches social skills like sharing, cooperation and following instructions—but team sports do this more effectively.

There are also health and hygiene risks. What's to stop kids coughing or sneezing over the food? Cleanliness is another concern. Little hands touch everything, not only the food and utensils but the classroom facilities as well.

Just check the TV guide if you want to see real cooking. There are cooking shows for everyone from beginners to gourmets: step-by-step recipes you can follow in your own home without the chaotic conditions of a workspace.

Finally, my parents didn't have cooking classes. They certainly don't feel disadvantaged. It's time to get back to proper lessons at school and leave the fun activities to be done at home.

Please note that this sample has not been written under test conditions. During a test you might not have the time to produce such a polished piece of writing. However, this sample gives you a standard to aim for.

Language and ideas

Vocabulary

Good use is made of unusual words; adverbs of time, verbs and adjectives.

A strong positive tone is used to state the writer's case.

Colloquial terms are used to help the reader identify with the argument.

Sentence structure

A wide variety of sentence beginnings is used.

Most sentences are statements, with a mixture of simple and compound sentences.

Ideas

Exclamation is used for dramatic effect.

Ideas are well articulated to create a sense of rational, logical argument.

Rhetorical questions keep the reader engaged.

Questions are used to highlight the writer's frustrations.

Punctuation

Controlled use is made of exclamations and italics.

Exclamation marks are used to increase the sense of urgency in making a decision.

Other punctuation, including apostrophes, commas and full stops, is correctly applied.

Spelling

There are no spelling errors of common or unusual words.

Language and ideas

Vocabulary

Good use is made of unusual words, adverbs of time, verbs and adjectives.

A reflective tone describes the visit.

Informal language helps the reader identify with the writer.

Sentence structure

A wide variety of sentence beginnings are included.

Most sentences are statements with a mixture of compound and simple sentences.

Ideas

Exclamations are used for dramatic effect.

Similes give a clear picture of the writer's annoyance.

Initials are used correctly (SUV).

Ideas are well articulated and sequenced to create a sense of relevant observations.

Specific location facts and names keep the reader engaged.

Punctuation

Controlled use is made of exclamations and italics.

Other punctuation, including commas, apostrophes and full stops, is correctly applied.

Spelling

There are no spelling errors of common, unusual or technical words.

Writing Test 4: sample answer

A visit to Inskip Point

On the first Monday of our holiday at Rainbow Beach, while I was having breakfast Dad declared we should have a look around Inskip Point. It could be interesting, I'd never heard of Inskip Point. It sounded like a kindergarten playground. I hoped it wasn't too far.

It could be a fun idea as the day was cloudy and breezy and anything to do in the water would get uncomfortable quite quickly.

We left our holiday cottage about ten and headed up the coast. Along the way I watched the passing scenery. Through the spindly coastal scrub, I caught glimpses of the wide beaches and the deep blue water of the Coral Sea. Between the road and the beaches there were bushy camping grounds and crowded caravan parks. At one stage we were overtaken by a dusty trio of SUVs all sporting fishing rods on their hoods or racks on the bonnets. Mum made the comment that the fishing must be good up here!

Dad sucked in his lips. It was his way of saying he wished they'd slow down a bit as the swirling sand that had encroached from the scrub onto the road made driving less than pleasant.

Finally the bitumen came to an end and we had to leave our car in a carpark and walk to the point.

The SUVs could continue over a deeply sandy track. It became evident to me that the point was the end of a narrow peninsula pointing towards Fraser Island, a kilometre north of the beach. Two ferries linked Inskip Point and the island during the day.

After a short walk we emerged from the scrub. In the distance I could see a ferry that would transport vehicles across to Fraser Island where beach driving was permitted.

I didn't need to be told to keep off the deeply rutted tracks. A stream of SUVs roared and rumbled and swerved across the open beach, sending sprays of sand into the air. The wide Inskip Point expanse of sand looked like a battle zone.

I could smell the sea—and the fumes from engines growling across the deep sand like angry monsters!

Mum made a disapproving *hmmm* sound and Dad muttered something.

This was no kindergarten playground!

Please note that this sample has not been written under test conditions. During a test you might not have the time to produce such a polished piece of writing. However, this sample gives you a standard to aim for.

Structure

Audience

The topic is one that would be familiar to students and parents.

The writer firmly establishes the who, what and where of the topic.

The recount is written in the first person (I, our).

Text structure

Points are organised sequentially.

The text contains a well-organised introduction, support points and a conclusion.

Positive words used throughout the text provide contrast (hopefully, pleasant).

Paragraphing

A new paragraph is used for each new point.

A topic sentence introduces the paragraph's main idea.

Cohesion

The writer's intention is established early.

The writer refers regularly to words used in the question topic.

The recount is written in the past tense.

Personal experience bolsters the position taken.

The final paragraph refers to the topic and re-establishes how the writer's feelings evolved.

The recount ends with the writer's implied opinion.

The concluding sentence rounds off the recount by referring to the playground mentioned in the introduction.